Bloody Justice

𝔅𝔩𝔬𝔬𝔡𝔶 𝔍𝔲𝔰𝔱𝔦𝔠𝔢

THE TRUTH BEHIND THE BANDIDO MASSACRE AT SHEDDEN

ANITA ARVAST

John Wiley & Sons Canada, Ltd.

Library and Archives Canada Cataloguing in Publication Data

Arvast, Anita
  Bloody justice : the truth behind the Bandido massacre at Shedden / Anita Arvast.

Includes index.
ISBN 978-1-118-15651-3

  1. Mass murder—Ontario—Shedden. 2. Bandidos (Gang).
3. Motorcycle gangs—Ontario. 4. Trials (Murder)—Ontario—London.
I. Title.

HV6535.C3A78 2012   364.152'340971334   C2012-900456-

ISBN 978-1-11815743-5 (ebk); 978-1-11815745-9 (ebk);
978-1-11815746-6 (ebk)

Production Credits
Cover design: Ian Koo
Interior text design: Laserwords
Typesetter: Laserwords
Printer: Trigraphik | LBF

John Wiley & Sons Canada, Ltd.
6045 Freemont Blvd.
Mississauga, Ontario
L5R 4J3

Printed in Canada
1 2 3 4 5 LBF TRI 16 15 14 13 12

*To those who strive for social justice in
all walks of life.*

CONTENTS

ACKNOWLEDGEMENTS

In 2008 I was looking for a new writing project.

I had grown tired of researching and writing in the academic arena, typically journal articles that are read by a miniscule percentage of the population but consume so much of a professor's time. The articles don't, in my opinion, have much of an impact on our society.

I had been reading about the Bandidos case and an acquaintance of mine suggested I might be interested in writing about it. I had never followed a trial before or been inside a jail. It could be an adventure.

I moved to London where the trial was being held, scoured over preliminary hearing transcripts, reviewed testimonies and forensic evidence, and travelled a couple of times a week to meet with one of the accused.

It was indeed an adventure—one that would profoundly alter my understanding of justice.

There are many people who have contributed to this project.

I do not thank the one police officer who banished me from court for two weeks for providing literature and a thesaurus to Brett Gardiner through all of the proper channels. I also do not thank his supervisor for supporting this perspective that I proved to be some sort of a threat. I do thank Justice Heeney for having that settled and those police officers who smiled at me when I was permitted to return.

I thank my family for their support and for (mostly) not complaining about my considerable time away from home and behind my computer screen.

I thank the many lawyers who shared their time and expertise, and met my befuddlement with patience and humour. I congratulate my many bench mates who managed to sit through the trial with me on less-than-comfortable seating.

At various stages of this project, I have been supported by outstanding editors: Martha Sharpe, Don Loney, Brian Will, and Carol Harrison. The team at Wiley is just that: a team.

Finally, this book could not have been written without the many personal stories shared by Brett and his family.

•   •   •

Author's Note

The author obtained all material in this book from attendance through the criminal trial and review of transcripts. In addition, she met regularly with Brett Gardiner in the detention centre to hear about his life story. According to biker culture, one may never divulge any information about the motorcycle club or any of its activities. Brett remained true to that code and only ever divulged information about his life before the events at Shedden. All content in this book is based heavily on the trial and testimony.

Some names have been altered to protect family members and children.

CAST OF CHARACTERS

Murdered

Jamie "Goldberg" Flanz, 37
George "Pony" Jessome, 52
George "Crash" Kriarakis, 28
John "Boxer" Muscedere, 48
Luis "Chopper" Raposo, 41
Frank "Bammer" Salerno, 43
Paul "Big Pauly" Sinopoli, 30
Michael "Little Mikey" Trotta, 31

Convicted

Includes ages at time of arrest

Marcelo Aravena (1 count manslaughter; 7 counts first degree), 30

Brett "Bull" Gardiner (2 counts manslaughter; 6 counts first degree), 21

Wayne "Weiner" Kellestine (8 counts first degree), 56

Frank Mather (1 count manslaughter; 7 counts first degree), 32

Dwight "D" Mushey (8 counts first degree), 36

Eric Niessen (1 count of obstruction of justice—pleaded guilty), 45

Michael "Taz" Sandham (8 counts first degree), 36

Informant

MH

Crown Prosecution

Kevin Gowdey
Fraser Kelly

Judges

Mr. Justice Thomas Heeney—Superior Court (oversaw trial)
Mr. Justice Ross Webster—Superior Court (oversaw preliminary inquiry)

Defence

For Marcelo Aravena

Tony Bryant
Kathryn Wells

For Brett Gardiner

Christopher Hicks
Bella Petrouchinova

For Wayne Kellestine

Clay Powel
Ken McMillan

For Frank Mather

Greg Leslie
Rob Lockhart

For Dwight Mushey

Michael Moon
Christian Angelini

For Michael Sandham

Gordon Cudmore
Don Crawford

Others

Merv Breaton, former bank robber and alleged trafficker

Marty Angenent, purveyor of the Holland House

Ron Burling—Hells Angels member

Officer Tim Dyack—Winnipeg police officer with whom MH first works as an informant

Detective Constable Jeff Gateman—member of the Ontario Provincial Police Biker Enforcement Unit and one of MH's "handlers"

Detective Sergeant Mark Loader—member of the Ontario Provincial Police Biker Enforcement Unit and one of MH's "handlers"

Constable Scott Rossiter—police officer shot in head

David O'Neil—suspect in Rossiter's murder found in shallow grave behind Kellestine's farm

Russ "Rusty" and Mary Steele—owners of property where cars are found

"Preacher"—Pilgrims member who tried to convert bikers to Christianity

The names of Brett Gardiner's family have all been changed

CHAPTER 1

Assembling the Chorus

As flies to wanton boys are we to th' gods.

—*King Lear*, act 4, scene 1

Russ "Rusty" Steele and Mary Steele generally rise each morning at 7:15. On the morning of April 8, 2006, they had finished their breakfast cereal and were topping up their coffees as they sat in their kitchen overlooking Stafford Line. Their house is nestled among pine trees just outside of Shedden, Ontario, invariably described as "a sleepy hamlet" about 20 miles west of London, but they still had a clear view of the gravel road that runs from their house back into town. Just then Forbes Holden drove past, likely on one of his regular visits to the Steeles' neighbour, Charlie McMullen. Mary always said they could set their watches by Forbes's visits.

Shortly after 8 a.m. the Steeles got a call from Charlie. "Forbes tells me there's a mess out near your field. A bunch of cars out there. We're going out for a look-see."

The Steeles live on what is typically considered a "gentleman's farm." Their substantial brick home is relatively new. The grounds are immaculately kept with a circular gravel driveway, parking spaces for numerous vehicles, and a pond that is inviting to look upon with birch trees settled on its shores and an arched bridge separating the deeper from the shallower sections. During the summer, the pond is green and murky, with a bottom you likely do not want to feel underfoot. On this spring day, however, the pond is merely a grey, thawing slush. By country standards, where the sounds are subdued by the perching larks, a breeze across willows, the gentle flap of a Canadian flag tethered to its pole, this is decidedly a pond for reflection as opposed to swimming or fishing. This is a place that exudes calm. When you approach the driveway and turn off the car, there is nothing more pressing than this peace.

Behind the pond and the main house, the property spans 95 acres of treed and harvested land. A deer run erected by the previous owners runs from the road to the barn and out toward the end of the property along Stafford Line. Eight-foot-tall deer-and-buffalo fencing differentiates the traditional cattle farmers from the entrepreneurial and aspiring. The Steeles wouldn't have much use for such fencing.

The Steeles are salt-of-the earth retired dairy farmers. They moved here the previous fall for "the peace and quiet." Like most people who decide to live in the country or have grown up rural all their lives, they wanted to be somewhat removed from broader society but still be part of a community. This is, after all, a place where grandchildren come and play, and a place to mix the odd euchre tournament with substantial seclusion. It is a place to relax after so many years of running the dairy farm—arduous work in the seeding, fielding, and eventual recovery of crops set against dairy cattle that need multiple daily feedings and milkings, not to mention the spring calving.

Before moving here just six months ago, the couple sold off their dairy farm in Kintore, another small town just 20 minutes on the other side of London. There they had raised the much-admired red-and-white Holsteins, first seen as an abomination to dairy farmers then embraced in the late 1980s as high fashion. Their five-time all-American champion Holstein, Stelbro Renita Range, long since passed away, is remembered in a plaster and painted one-foot-tall casting. Despite the outbreak of mad-cow disease, the Steeles were able to sell their healthy stock for a good price and move to this spacious new home near Shedden.

The Steeles don't yet know the neighbours particularly well, but they do know Charlie and Forbes. The Steeles consider two scenarios. Perhaps Charlie is pulling a prank and they will arrive to find one of his jokes greeting them; both Charlie and Forbes are regular pranksters. Or maybe some local teenagers took a joy ride to the next level, which sometimes happens in the country. By the glint in Rusty's eye, you can tell he favours the first scenario. Either way, this isn't an emergency; the couple sips the remains of their coffee then drives to where a tow truck and three other cars sit close to the side road in a tractor's lane-way beside dense brush. Charlie and Forbes are already on the scene, warming their hands by the truck's interior defroster fans.

The first car they see is a grey Infiniti, backed into the unused deer run, seemingly abandoned. That's the only one that looks like someone tried to park. The rest are all run aground in the thick mud of the field.

The tow truck is especially peculiar as it has a car attached to its hoist and seems to have just run off the shoulder. Even odder is the Toronto identification and phone number sten-cilled across its sides. Couldn't be local teenagers, the couple deduce. Must be city kids. A whack of them.

Rusty and Mary try to peek inside one of the vehicles, but a blanket obstructs their view. The other vehicles are heavily frosted over and fail to provide any immediate clues. Mary thinks one of the trunks is slightly ajar, but can't be sure. She is now beginning to wonder who might be around the neighbourhood and why they'd abandon these vehicles. The couple has watched enough television programs depicting criminal discoveries that their curiosity turns to concern. Forbes tells them that as he drove by that morning he could make out two men running away through the field.

"Good luck to them fellows getting back to Toronto in that direction," he chuckles as he points south over the field.

Mary is a little more serious. "Don't touch anything," she warns Rusty. "You don't want to disturb any evidence."

This represents a bit of excitement on Stafford Line and a chance for the couple to practise something of a vicarious interest in forensics. They return home and dial 911 for the police. Curious and unknowing, they drive back to the scene. They haven't ruled out that this is likely nothing more than kids weary of winter and hopped up on whisky, out for a joy ride in "borrowed" vehicles. Rusty approaches the vehicles as Mary sits by the side of the road; then Rusty yells out the licence plate numbers as she scribbles them onto a pad of paper they carry in their glove compartment, trying to shush her husband at the same time. He heeds his wife and is careful not to disturb evidence, or to awaken the presumed occupants who are probably "sleeping it off" and will likely be a little cranky when they wake up. That is Mary's biggest concern: What if they wake up or someone comes back? Charlie and Forbes stand by and make small talk.

The Steeles head back to the house and phone the police again since they have discovered another car farther in the field: a total of four vehicles now. Then the couple goes back to the side of the road to wait. Inside their vehicle. Just in case. Charlie and Forbes join them.

It isn't long before an Ontario Provincial Police cruiser with its one constable arrives. Officer Karl Johnston was dispatched at 8:22 and arrives within 10 minutes. He peers inside the semi-open window and sees a man with wounds to his face. As per protocol, he immediately contacts Emergency Medical Services and calls his detachment to send backup. He waits by his vehicle until the second officer and car arrive. By 9 a.m. he is joined by Officer Jeff Chandelier and they look out over the field and the vehicles, tracing their steps and being careful not to disturb any potential evidence. As one of the officers opens the slightly ajar hatch, he calls out to the other officer, "Body." He approaches the grey Infiniti next and peers in to see a male in the rear passenger side. "Body."

The officers are soon joined by ambulance attendant Lee Restorick, who checks the pulse and notices the coolness of the man in the rear of the Infiniti. Rigor mortis has set in. Lee then approaches the semi-open hatch and confirms with the officers that they are dealing with multiple deaths.

Mary and Rusty stand looking on in bewilderment. Two guys stuffed in a trunk? The two officers then guide Mary, Rusty, Charlie, and Forbes back to their vehicles and ask them to return to their homes.

"Come by for lunch," Charlie tells the Steeles, "Kay's fixing up some egg salad sandwiches."

Just after 9 a.m., as helicopters whirl above, Mary and Rusty go to the local OPP detachment to provide their statements. Forbes goes and gives his statement: "I just saw the cars and two guys running south through the field."

Mary phones one of their daughters before heading to the detachment and leaves a voice-mail message: "We found some bodies on the property, but we're okay." As a long-time dairy farmer, Mary is accustomed to being matter-of-fact.

After giving their statements at the police station, the Steeles head back to Kay and Charlie McMullen's house for the promised egg salad sandwiches and coffee. By now the Internet is awash with what has really been found on the site and Charlie and Kay say the neighbours are phoning to ask about the eight bodies.

"Eight?" Mary and Rusty shake their heads. "Holy cow."

The Steeles finish their sandwiches and return home. By early afternoon there is a central command set up just at the end of their driveway. Once inside they discover 56 voicemail messages, a few from friends but most from media as far away as London, England.

Mary's only other contact with police was several years ago at their Kintore farm. At 2 a.m. she drove out to check on one of her cows that was ready to calve. She parked her truck close to the barn and left its lights on. Shortly after, two uniformed officers showed up with guns drawn on her. Though initially startled, she quickly took control and advantage of the situation. "You guys look strong," she said. "Why don't you come here and help pull." They pulled the calf out and kept the exhausted Mary waiting with them until they could see the calf stand. Mary sat on one of the stools shaking her head. She had seen many a calf stand and wanted to simply return to bed, but she obliged the officers who would eventually buy "Opie" as their mascot. At a time when many farmers were losing their hard-earned lands to bank foreclosures, many with considerable reluctance, the police force was in dire need of some positive publicity.

These circumstances were considerably different. Typically not easily shaken, the Steeles were frightened. They were relieved that their old dog, Winston, had not heard anything in the night. Had he barked, Mary would definitely have risen and gone out with a flashlight to see what was happening. And then who knows what might have happened?

Encroaching brush separates the Steeles' farmhouse from the field of discovery, as does a subdued set of pines that distinguish the gentleman from the work. Thankfully these trees are probably what saved old Winston. That and failing hearing.

Suddenly this mix of harvested, lost, entangled, and discriminately contained farmland is a central meeting point for hundreds of journalists, investigators, writers, and curious neighbours. By late afternoon, more than 150 police officers are on the scene. Some arrive from nearby St. Thomas where they had been attending murder victim Lynne Harper's gravesite as her remains had been returned to their place of rest. (After 35 years, forensics couldn't prove that Steven Truscott, the 14-year old boy charged with her murder and sentenced to be hanged in 1959, was either guilty or innocent. The death penalty had eventually been commuted to life imprisonment. It would be more than a year after the forensic entomology was done that the courts would overturn his conviction.)

Other police officers arrive from the Caledonia reserve where a land dispute is taking place between natives and developers. One hundred and fifty police officers at the end of the driveway isn't the attention anyone choosing to live in a quiet countryside expects or wants, even if the drama of the early part of the day was somewhat exciting.

Eight men's bodies were found in the vehicles: one rolled up in an old carpet in the trunk of a car with numerous bullet wounds and the rest of the men slumped over or curled up in various seats with execution-style gun wounds to the head.

Who were these guys? What did they do to wind up like this?

Many a conversation occurs today in the aisles of Palmer's Supermarket and Paint Store less than a mile from the discovery of the bodies. There is some talk of a motorcycle club called the Bandidos.

"What are the Bandidos?" Forbes asks Charlie. "I never heard of them."

Legal officials around the world in countries that have Bandidos membership—the United States, Canada, Sweden, Australia, Germany, and Britain to name a few—regard the Bandidos as a highly organized and violent culture

of motorcycle gang members participating in numerous criminal activities. Did these guys fit the bill?

Within a couple of days, monuments were erected at
the site by the victims' next of kin: a white cross with a small
fence around it; a blue spruce; some orange chrysanthemums;
and, at one point, a Toronto Maple Leafs jersey with the
number 93. Doug "Killer" Gilmour must have been a hero
to one of the men.

"Remember those biker wars in Quebec," neighbour Paul
Severs says adamantly. "We don't want any of that shit here.
I hope they are all gone . . . either dead or going to prison."

"Kill each other and go to jail," offers his sidekick as they
stand in the aisle of Palmer's. "It's all good."

Once the media lets the world know about the discovery,
sentiments pour in. The comments page on the Canadian
Broadcasting Corporation's (CBC's) website conveys what
most people are thinking.

"Eight dead Bandidos . . . what's the problem?"

"Who cares, let them kill each other."

"I favour the Government of Canada legally eliminating
every one of these useless carcasses, using the authority given
to our military to deal with terrorists."

One quote receives the iconic "thumbs up" approval from
112 of its 130 readers: "Good riddance to bad rubbish."

Mary and Rusty just sit back, shaking their heads. They
don't judge. They just feel badly for all those families. And
oddly blessed that with something so horrible happening
on their property, they are protected by whatever gods are
watching over them.

CHAPTER 2

The Man Who Would Be King

The prince of darkness is a gentleman.

—*King Lear*, act 3, scene 4

The entire region around London, Ontario, is named according to British tradition. There is Middlesex County, Elgin County, Southwold, Strathroy, and Dutton. Just about every concession and road in the area tips its hat to English lineage.

Maybe this is why Wayne Kellestine chose to live in the area. Kellestine wasn't the least bit like Rusty, Mary, Charlie, and Forbes. He was a man with ambition. And maybe he was fated to live a Shakespearian tragedy, a modern-day King Lear in this makeshift Britain.

Talbot Line is one of the few concessions to a specifically Canadian history. Thomas Talbot emigrated from Ireland in the late 1700s. As the personal secretary of John Graves

Simcoe and essentially the author of modern roads with his efforts to remove both Crown and clergy reserves from main throughways, Talbot quickly assumed a position of power in the community. He was celebrated locally for bringing wealth to the region via the eponymous Talbot Trail, but not well understood in terms of his contributions to the 1837 Upper Canada Rebellion. It seems that the colonel preferred to give land only to settlers he liked; if they fell out of favour, he would simply erase their pencilled names from the documents and take their land back. Aside from such a small and little-known reference to Canadian history, London, Ontario, seems desperate to be London, England.

About a seven-minute drive along the Talbot Line from Shedden is a significantly smaller town, Iona Station. It has just a handful of houses and one business, the Holland House, which was one of Wayne's favourite haunts.

The Holland House is an interesting establishment—a restaurant, tavern, gift and antique shop, used bookstore, and sales point for Edam cheese, blue-and-white Dutch ceramic tiles, and eBay auction paraphernalia.

Marty Angenent, a man in his early 60s with a penchant for ball caps, had been running the establishment for some 25 years when the bodies were discovered near Shedden. As a former maître d' with some of the finest hotels and restaurants in Canada, he had come to this small town to have a place of his own that reflected and celebrated his Dutch heritage. He prided himself on never serving patrons more than two servings of beer. He made strong coffee. He seemed to be okay with fat, lazy house flies in the windows. He liked history and acquiring more than just a superficial understanding of anything from politics and law to agriculture and sports. His ex-wife and kids didn't have much use for him, but he was happy with his lot in life.

The Holland House looks and smells like a grandparent's attic, with mouldy books, vinyl office and kitchen chairs from the 1960s, plastic table cloths, and dusty vases on just about any horizontal surface. It's also a place where everyone seems to know each other's name, but isn't interested in each other's business. Farmers, business people, suburbanites, and even the odd motorcycle rider are all welcome here.

Marty remembers Friday, April 7, 2006, like it was yesterday.

The Holland House had just a handful of regulars that night enjoying a plate of fish and chips, the Friday-night specialty, washed down with a pint and followed up with a cup of freshly brewed coffee. The usual topics were discussed: what the *Farmer's Almanac* was predicting for the upcoming season, who had won Thursday's hockey game, what was on television.

If it was relatively quiet at the Holland House, it was even quieter out at the Iona Station intersection itself. One stoplight. One business. About six houses.

The Holland House sits on Iona Line, which stretches north to south across the major throughway from London to Windsor and indeed from central Canada to central United States, Highway 401. Exiting the 401 and driving north on Iona Line, the second road that one comes to is Aberdeen Line. The entranceway from Iona Line to Aberdeen Line is flanked on both sides by Cowal-McBride Cemetery. Gravestones date back to the 1800s. Many of the locals have generations of ancestors resting here.

Apparently, it was far less quiet on Aberdeen Line than it was at either the Holland House or the graveyard.

Wayne lived on Aberdeen Line and he was always up for a good party. About a half a mile west down the road from the graveyard was his farmhouse, far less the stately ideal of

farming than the Steeles' residence near Shedden. A two-storey
white wooden home, it was expansive, but long overdue for
maintenance. Nevertheless, the fields were just as serene and
the family residing there, Wayne and Tina Kellestine, along
with their young daughter, Kassie, wanted a life removed
from traditional society. The house sported a large and amply
furnished living room, complete with a traditional stone
fireplace. Off this room was a games room, including a pool
table and hot tub. But the plumbing wasn't really working, so
now the hot tub sat empty and the toilets needed to be flushed
"manually" with buckets of water. The family couldn't drink
the well water because of the presence of E. coli, so they had
to purchase bottled water in bulk.

Wayne had lived here for about 30 years. In its heyday,
the house was home to some of the finest parties, with beer
flowing, the pool table hopping, a band pumping out old-time
rock and roll and an army of men hugging each other with the
traditional greeting of "Love you, Bro." In those days, money
was easy and friendship was forever.

Journalists from the city would eventually write about this
house as a "mess," but most local farmers would appreciate that
the family living here celebrated its history with photographs
along its walls, collectibles scattered throughout the home,
and a wide selection of tools and parts in the garage and basement available for any do-it-yourself project. Working farms
are indeed messy, but the contents at this farm differed from
the traditional working type. There were a couple of police
scanners. Photos of motorcycles adorned just about every
room. There were hundreds of videos of drunken parties with
rough-looking men.

Then there were the videos of Wayne himself, either a king
or a jester—you couldn't be certain—who deemed himself
indestructible and whom you didn't dare cross. He danced
a jig, he sang songs out of key; he bantered on while filming

his brothers. He even videotaped a man raping a woman on the pool table and then had the audacity to keep the footage rolling as the woman sat crying.

Reporters would tell of Wayne's sensational side, but he also had a cache of standard family movies: friends together playing with children, his daughter's first steps, loving footage of Tina's devotion in which Wayne told her of his undying love for her. In the years that followed, nobody would hear about the many videos in which Wayne showed himself a loving father and devoted husband.

At the outer perimeter of the residence, a fence lined the property with old stone pillars that secured a heavy, rusted iron gate—an aged but operational surveillance camera perched on one of the pillars, its sights fixed on the road. The 100-or-so-year-old maples and oaks that ran along the road had been cut down a few years ago to provide Wayne a better view of Aberdeen Line.

There were four Doberman pinschers, each with its own doghouse, chained up close to the first fence around the property. None of them were neutered to ensure their testosterone was high. There was a second, significantly higher fence that enclosed the house and barn topped with barbed wire. And there was a *lot* of Nazi memorabilia: helmets, plates, mortar shells, flags, and an "SS" sign on the barn, the logo from an old biker gang called the Annihilators led by none other than Wayne.

Only by plane would you be able to discern a swastika cut out in the field. Only by historic surveillance would one be interpreting the sorts of gatherings that previously occurred at this farm, not of white supremacists but that more than a few locals knew involved motorcycle clubs. Some of the locals welcomed the protection afforded them. After all, bikers would scare away common robbers. Wayne and his biker friends weren't scary to the neighbouring farmers.

He had the finest pig roasts in the area and could always be counted on to have some cold beer on hand. Despite the video, men forcing themselves on women would certainly not be the norm.

Wayne always said hello. Always smiled. Always waved.

But if you were out in his field, he knew about it and wanted to know who you were and what you were doing on his property. This was Wayne's world. Nobody came on it without an invitation. Fair enough. His neighbours didn't wander out there and the one crop surveyor who did never did it again. Not that he was hurt. He was just met by Wayne's mean look, eyes that would stare through your soul and make you regret being born. Wayne saved that look for people he perceived as a threat.

He never looked on his neighbours this way if they were respecting his property. He looked on them with kindness.

Marty Angenent had come to count on Wayne as a protective force in the community. He was a regular patron of the Holland House, always generous with the staff, amiable with the patrons, and charitable with Marty. And Wayne's demented sense of humour was legendary, always welcomed by the staff and patrons. Here was a man who loved life.

At one point many years prior, Marty recounted numerous break-and-enters to his establishment and Wayne ensured that he would prevent any such further criminal activity. Money was never exchanged for this protection; it was a gentleman's agreement between two men who respected each other's right to run a business.

Marty could sum up his impression of Wayne pretty easily. "People talked about him, but I never asked. To me he was always a fair and generous man with a good sense of humour. And a better sense of loyalty."

• • •

At the Kellestine farm, the flags and memorabilia were perhaps appropriately vilified by many and understood by few outside of the organization. In the Annihilators' anti-racist beginnings, the Nazi ephemera served as crude anti-establishment symbols; but in a socially conservative society, it came to be seen as merely representing hatred, intolerance, and violence. In the world of motorcycle clubs, Nazi paraphernalia does not connote Nazi sympathies; the flags, symbols, and songs serve to express a rejection of society and particularly its policing. Legal officials are systematically seen as soldiers of anti-civilian regimes, whereas bikers are freedom fighters. In fact, it is in some ways a highly complex culture of civil libertarians that is ironically paramilitary, though it is rarely depicted as such by the media or understood as such by the general public.

In the case of Wayne Kellestine, who called his entrepreneurial security business KKK Securities and signed off e-mails with the occasional Nazi code for "killer" (SS), the simplistic interpretation of the symbols of white supremacy at his farm may have been in order, but then again, Wayne was always a far more complex individual than meets the eye. Pretty sure the Toronto Maple Leafs hockey captain, Doug "Killer" Gilmour didn't sign his hockey cards with an SS.

On the farmhouse door was a popular rendering of the Latin phrase, *Caedite eos. Novit enim Dominus qui sunt eius* ("Kill 'em all. Let God sort 'em out"). Somehow the saying was acceptable when used by the U.S. Marines or the British Green Berets and worn as a motto on their T-shirts. But was it acceptable for a motorcycle enthusiast with a sordid past?

The Kellestine home held more than just Nazi trappings. Despite two lifetime bans for owning weapons, Wayne had quite the stash of guns.

So just who was Wayne Kellestine? He was a man with a violent and yet tragic history and one who would never go down without a fight to the finish. Hitler was his arch hero and drugs were apparently his greatest allies and adversaries, regularly fuelling an already unstable mindset. Cocaine and methamphetamines ("speed" in these circles) would provide euphoric courage in their initial usage. But addictions have a way of turning something once pleasurable into something immanently painful. Wayne was in pain, but he had not arrived here overnight.

Historically he was a man to be feared, but he was also regarded as a keen leader. Depending on whom you asked, his reputation ranged from being a renegade idealist to a raving lunatic. Regardless, nobody wanted to be on his bad side except for his rivals the Hells Angels, some of whom had attempted to take Wayne's life on various occasions.

In his younger days, he made good money running drugs, pimping strippers, and stealing, and he had earned a reputation as a killer, though no murders were ever traced to him; some think he just wanted to have the reputation without doing the work to earn it. A couple of bodies had surfaced close to his place. Much of the gossip typically circled around the finding of a body near Kellestine's property—a man wanted in the murder of Ingersoll police officer Scott Rossiter. Some 15 years prior to the events of April 2006, David O'Neil's body was found in a shallow grave with three bullet wounds to the head from a .38 calibre revolver. Though Kellestine was never charged as the killer, word around the Holland House maintained that he had at least led police to the dumping ground. O'Neil was found off a path near the Kellestine farm that only a couple of people could have known about. His body was buried from the neck down, with the head remaining above ground as some sort of message. O'Neil wasn't liked by either police or bikers. He was a cop-killer and a potential rat. Bikers don't kill cops. It brings on too much attention. But they do kill rats.

Wayne's charges for having shot at a rival biker near his home in 1991 were dropped shortly after the finding of

O'Neil's body and speculation remains that his charges were dropped because he may have led police to the body. So while Wayne did a lot of time in jail, it was never for murder. It seems authorities just couldn't or didn't want to pin him for this.

When he shopped at the local farmers' co-op, Wayne only ever bought the best dog food for his prized Dobermans, pulling out wads of $100 bills from his pocket and skimming a couple from the top, with a dagger hanging from his belt buckle. Local resident John Tunks had seen him at the co-op frequently and laughed that nobody else could have gotten away with carrying such a big knife in public. Even though Wayne served many years in prison, the law didn't mess with him on some of these "petty" issues that would see most citizens facing charges in court.

Those who knew Wayne well knew that he had something called "my list." If you wronged him in a substantial way, he took the notebook out of his pocket and made a point of writing your name down and saying, "You're on my list." It might take him 15 or 20 years to strike back, but if you were on the list you could be sure he would eventually find you and exact whatever justice he thought you deserved. There are lots of bikers with brawn and bravado. Wayne had the far more lethal combination of bravado and brains—and an absence of remorse.

● ● ●

Kellestine's loss of this status as a biker of envy came slowly and painfully.

By 2006, Wayne was down on his luck. He seldom went to visit Marty at the Holland House, and when he did, he couldn't maintain the same generosity with the staff that he had once had. Despite his decades leading various bike gangs, including recently serving as an executive member with the Canadian

Bandidos club after his Annihilators gang ceased to exist, his brothers didn't want to hang out with him anymore. He was hopped up on drugs and had become increasingly paranoid, posing a danger to his brothers, even though some of them were also battling some serious addictions.

His world was now a disaster. The skeletons of old cars and rusted sheds that littered his property and the surveillance equipment and barbed fences were just an outward reflection of a man gone mad. His long, stringy silver hair straggled down his thin frame while his pot belly hung out over his old jeans. He needed glasses now to see. And he had a cough that he could never shake, something that sounded like a wounded coyote.

Photos of him at various public events depicted a crazed and aged biker who alternatively danced a jig, broke into the German national anthem, and even ate raccoon and deer feces. In other videos he could be seen drinking beer with his buddies and giving them loving hugs. And then there were the photos where his menacing appearance and stony eyes could send a chill up the most courageous person's spine. Wayne was clearly not a man to be messed with.

In the videos he now filmed of himself, he was a tempest in the body of an old, abused, and now discarded shell.

So what does a man do when he wants to regain his sense of importance? How does a dismissed renegade return to royalty? If he were logical, he might slay his enemies; if he were tragic, he would slay his allies.

CHAPTER 3

And All the King's Men Couldn't

Man's life is cheap as beast's.

—*King Lear*, act 2, scene 4

On the night of April 7, 2006, two police detachments had been parked near the Kellestine farm. Surveillance was standard for Wayne's place, and on this night one of the detachments followed a car heading there. In the car was a man suspected of murdering a drug dealer.

The police may have been there the entire night. Certainly the folks in the neighbourhood thought this to be true, but they would only whisper it for fear of reprisal. After all, any reasonable person would not want to get on Wayne's bad side.

But the bodies found near the Steele farm presented some fairly substantial evidence. First, murder was obvious from the beginning. Once the bodies were identified as members or affiliates of the Toronto Bandidos biker gang, the investigation quickly focused on the Kellestine farm.

Within a few hours of the Shedden discovery, at 12:40 on the afternoon of April 8, the police began watching the Kellestine farm more intensely. At about 3 p.m. another vehicle arrived at the farm. The police stopped it briefly and learned that it contained a Bandido associate by the name of Eric Niessen and his common-law wife, Kerry Morris. Eric had been previously investigated because of concerns the police had that he was involved in drug dealing, specifically crystal meth, but his girlfriend was clean; she used to drive a cab for a local company and then worked at Tim Hortons so that she could spend more time with the children. Despite the surveillance, the officers let the couple pass through the gates, with Eric claiming that he had been partying with people at the Kellestine farm the night before and was today merely returning from a beer run. Had he known why the police were parked near the driveway, he probably would have steered clear. But it's probable that Wayne needed a little pick-me-up the day after a wild night of partying, and it's possible that Eric was there to help him.

By 5 p.m., a justice of the peace had granted a warrant to search the farm. The police quickly positioned themselves for the takedown.

A phone call was placed to Wayne by the police on surveillance. He eventually said he would come out only if the cops promised not to shoot his dogs, something that had happened in a previous arrest.

The five occupants were ordered to walk down the lengthy, gravel driveway, arms raised, without their jackets, while heavily armed officers trained their guns on them and aerial surveillance swept overhead.

They were then forced to kneel 66 feet from the end of the laneway leading up to the white homestead. Each individual was told to pull up his or her shirt to show that no weapons were concealed. They were handcuffed with plastic zip ties and led to awaiting police cruisers where they were put in the back seat and driven to various OPP detachments in and around London for questioning.

In keeping with his colourful reputation, Wayne had more than a strong disdain for police and typically wouldn't say anything to them. However, on the night that he was brought in for questioning, police video footage of the questioning showed him as the manic and compulsive caricature of someone on speed, even if the investigating police officer defined him later as "completely sober."

During questioning Wayne bantered like an obsessive compulsive. At one point the officers requested he give them his shoes. Wayne should have known better. He knew his rights; he should have spoken with or waited for his lawyer. And despite having endured hundreds of stops, detentions, and investigations in the past, he somehow forgot his rights that night. He gave up his shoes. The investigating officer left the room with them. After wandering the room, alternating standing, sitting, lying down, and repeating the words "fuck me," Wayne stared down at his feet in bewilderment.

"Where are my fucking shoes?" he muttered.

After a moment of reflection, it dawned on him.

"I gave them my fucking shoes."

"Why the fuck did I give them my fucking shoes?"

He sat back on the chair, putting his feet up on another chair.

"Fuck me." He ran his fingers through his stringy and greasy hair. "Fuck me."

At one point when the officers had left the room so that Wayne could call his wife, Tina, he claimed that the Hells Angels were clearly responsible. And then he told Tina that he had left her "script" for her. It seems unlikely they were writing a movie; more likely they were partners in whatever drugs Wayne had been consuming.

Another telephone conversation when the officers were out of the room seemed to confirm this. He merely said to Tina, "I got fucked up and I fucked up." These were the same words he had uttered to the now deceased John "Boxer" Muscedere's wife on the phone just before the arrest.

He would now be held in custody overnight and formally charged the next morning with eight counts of first-degree murder. By morning, he had apparently straightened up enough to talk to his lawyer.

Wayne wasn't the only one in for questioning, of course. Frank Mather had moved to the Kellestine farm a few days prior. He was a stoic middle-aged man with red hair fading into male pattern baldness and looks that spoke of his New Brunswick lineage tracing back to the fair-skinned Scots who settled there generations ago. He was at the Kellestine residence for a brief stay with his pregnant girlfriend in a makeshift bedroom in the basement, really just a mattress thrown on the floor of a dingy room strewn with spare parts, old tools, and creatures that crawled across the "bed" at night. Though possessing a lengthy criminal record for break-and-enters and possession back in New Brunswick, he had no history of violence. Frank and his girlfriend were merely migrants looking for a place to stay until they could figure out where they were going next. And Wayne had always been generous.

Frank's job in London didn't pan out, likely because he informed his boss's wife that her husband was having multiple affairs. It seems that even if Frank had a bit of a criminal history, he valued loyalty, and especially the vows of marriage.

He and his girlfriend didn't really know Wayne, even though a few would eventually contend that Frank had made the decision to join the biker culture and wanted to be part of a proposed chapter in the London area. That was all conjecture based on the fact that there was a photo of him at one of the Kellestine barbecues. But Frank wasn't the biker type. He just appreciated their generosity and their parties. On one occasion he had come to one of Wayne's parties but didn't have enough clothing for the several days of festivities. Someone gave him a "Bandido Supporter" T-shirt to wear, a shirt anyone at a Bandidos party would be permitted to have.

The third man kneeling on Aberdeen Line that day was Eric Niessen, who lived in nearby Perth County, what the police referred to as the meth capital of Ontario. But clearly his alleged involvement with drug trafficking was not the focus of the day. Though initially charged with murder, the charges would eventually be reduced to accessory after the fact and obstruction of justice, pleading guilty to the latter and being sentenced to two years.

The fourth of the accused was the only woman at the residence that day: Kerry Morris, Niessen's common-law wife. Her charges of murder would similarly be reduced to accessory after the fact and obstruction of justice, and then eventually withdrawn completely when her partner yielded to his charges.

Brett Gardiner, the youngest of the accused at a mere 21 years old, was the last to kneel on the driveway and make the trek to London in a cruiser. He also didn't fit the stereotype of a biker even if it was a lifestyle he periodically considered. He was a handsome and good-humoured young man with large, gentle, brown eyes. Despite the many tattoos that suggested he was a violent man, one knew from his eyes and demeanour that he really wasn't the tough guy he wanted others to think he was.

Though described in all of the media reports as "of no fixed address" because of something of a nomadic lifestyle in the previous six months, he had strong family ties in Calgary—his parents, his sister, his girlfriend and their young son. Like several of the accused and deceased, Brett didn't even own a motorcycle, a standard requirement for motorcycle-club membership. Sitting in the police station that night, Brett was terrified, but unable to expose his fear to anyone. He'd learned early on that you never show a weak side when dealing with cops and criminals. And since Wayne told him not to say anything, Brett kept his mouth shut over the several hours of accusative questioning.

For three hours the officers said they knew Brett was one of the murderers of the eight men. One of the officers said that his biker brothers had already incriminated him; he should just admit it. He was confused and frightened, but still didn't divulge knowing anything, as the presumably wiser Wayne had advised him.

He didn't know that Wayne was talking up a storm in his interview room. Mostly the demented ramblings of a guy still seriously screwed up on something, but occasionally offering up some insights. Brett was smart and frightened enough to merely shake his head during his interrogation. At the end of the three-hour interrogation, one officer said to Brett, "I bet you'd like to tell me to fuck off now." Since they didn't actually have any evidence, Brett was free to go.

Brett politely responded as his parents taught him. "It's been a pleasure meeting you."

He walked out the front doors of the London police station with nowhere to go, no sleep for two days, no coat, and too many troubles to count.

Brett meandered through the city night with just $20 (a gift he had received at the Kellestine farm from someone as yet unknown to the police), 10 cigarettes, a bit of tobacco, and some rolling papers to his name. Convinced he was being followed, he wandered somewhat aimlessly along a path that he thought was untraceable. He found a Tim Hortons coffee shop and bought a coffee, then ambled to the bus station where he phoned his parents. It was 11 p.m. in London,

9 p.m. in Calgary. His parents had already seen the news of the high-profile arrests at the farm and his mother gasped and cried when she heard his voice.

Brett needed to sound strong for them, but his emotions caught him a little off guard. His message was simple.

"Mom," he said followed by a lengthy pause. "I don't know nothing . . . I didn't see nothing . . . But I'm in deep shit."

His parents assured him there would be a ticket waiting for him at the bus station for the next bus to Calgary leaving the following morning at 10. He started walking. What would he do for the night? He held his head down and prayed as he walked. It was within the past year that he had become a born-again Christian. If he ever needed God, it was tonight. When he looked up, there was a bright light with the illuminated symbol of salvation. "Men's Mission," the sign read. There Brett settled in where he also had an opportunity to take stock of just how much trouble he was in. It now occurred to him that he was not likely to come out of this situation alive.

Eight bikers suddenly dead.

None of that was supposed to happen. His life had been at risk at the farmhouse. Surely his life was at even greater risk now. He was beyond exhaustion and well beyond thinking rationally, yet fuelled by the adrenaline that keeps a wild animal protected from predators. Indeed, he was a hunted man and even though he thought he successfully wove an untraceable path, he did not know the powers of those able to pursue him.

As he tried to settle on the bed, he reflected on not just the past day but the years leading up to it, and he wondered why his parents were always there for him no matter what he did.

Brett roamed to the washroom, rolled a cigarette, and ascended the steps to go back outside of the mission. His hands shook as he lit the cigarette and took long pulls that weren't having much of a calming effect. He wandered back to another pay phone where he called his parents collect. Both his parents each had a phone this time when he called. "Mom, Dad," he drew back tears as he drew in smoke. He exhaled. "I'm sorry I keep fucking up."

"Just come home, Brett," was the anxious response.

And then Brett said what he felt was absolutely critical on this night when he believed it certain that his life would be taken. "If I don't see you again, you have to know that I love you."

He hung up immediately, lit another cigarette, and returned to the mission where he hoped he would just be able to lie down for a while; sleep was certainly not an option until he was far away from this place and experience. But to lie down?

He wanted to rest, but even that would evade him. Instead, two police officers greeted him at the Mission and informed him he was being charged with eight counts of first-degree murder. Brett was shackled and taken to the Elgin-Middlesex Detention Centre on the outskirts of London. The cops didn't have evidence against him just an hour ago. What changed?

He was held in a cell. He could call an attorney, he was told. He had never faced serious charges before. Who would he call? Legal-aid options were explained to him. But how does one absorb this information when the pupils are dilated out of fear and exhaustion and the brain has shifted into that primordial fight-freeze-or-flee mode.

Charged with eight counts of first-degree murder. Never had a serious charge in his 21 years. Never spent much time outside of Alberta and now stuck in Ontario—a land with a completely different culture and morality. It might as well have been Istanbul.

Contrary to most people's understanding, a phone call is not an immediate entitlement in the Canadian legal system. It was a full two days before Brett was able to phone his parents again. When he did not pick up the ticket at the bus terminal and because of his parting words to them, they were certain he was dead.

There were a lot of people who would want Brett dead: Bandidos who felt threatened by his apparent knowledge of the organization even though he wasn't a member. Members seeking revenge. Bikers who knew he wasn't a biker and could become a turncoat for either opposing gangs or the cops. Hells Angels wanting to drop another rival. And then there was that generic public's perspective: Bikers killing bikers. Good riddance. Who cares if another biker dies?

Brett was a wannabe. He ranked lower than the lowest. As such, a man doesn't do anything and has the most at stake.

The one biker and these other so-called bikers—Wayne, Frank, and Brett—were deemed people to be abandoned with a grateful, albeit premature, dusting of the hands. The wannabe biker and the guy just living in the basement weren't even identified by rank as the people who had the most at stake. They were all just labelled as bikers.

• • •

Television trucks parked at the end of the Gardiner's driveway in Calgary and eyes turned toward the Gardiner family. Who are they? What had they done to create such a monster of a son? Oh, that poor family. Look what he's done to them.

Prior to this event, the Kellestine farm was little more than a curiosity. The raucous parties were only cause for shrugs. Now it was the scene of a substantial police investigation that would turn up stacks of weapons, cellphones, keys burned in a bonfire, and a stain on the barn floor caused by muriatic acid, a very strong cleaning solution. The investigators would even find a dead rabbit in the old freezer in the barn. But all of this was circumstantial evidence and the police knew they couldn't build a case just on that.

The neighbours were unable to offer up anything other than seeing the smoke from the bonfire.

"Those guys never bothered us," reported one of Kellestine's neighbours. "Wayne was always friendly. Always waved."

Another resident concurred. "In fact, to some degree you knew bad things weren't going to happen to us with these guys around."

Still other positions emerged. Some of the townsfolk from nearby Dutton said, "You never quite knew if you were going to get caught in some crossfire." They were referring to charges against Wayne Kellestine for gunfire that had taken place a few years before on the nearby Iona Road. Thomas Harmsworth, an ironic name for a fellow biker (and Kellestine's rival), took five bullets in the stomach but refused to testify against Kellestine. That refusal and the discovery of O'Neil's body allowed Kellestine to walk away from the charges in the shooting. On another occasion, two Hells Angels had tried to kill Wayne while he was out at the intersection just outside of the Holland House. Third-generation neighbouring farmer, John Tunks, referred to Wayne as something of a source of entertainment when he gathered with his friends at Iona Station. "He was always friendly and polite. But still we'd be asking if there was anything going on out at the Kellestine place. Just a bit of gossip to go with the grub."

Some of the other gossip in town centred on his 20-year-old daughter who had moved West and refused contact with her father, and his many lovers and girlfriends who looked like they had lived hard lives.

As the public awareness of the murders spread, there would others who would be disparaged. When Wayne's current wife Tina, a former stripper, went to Dutton for a loaf of bread or a box of cookies she would be met with prurient curiosity at best and derision at worst. She and her young daughter, Kassie, became objects to be stared at and feared. They were heroes in their survival, victims of circumstances, but ultimately *personae non gratae.*

Tina was avoided because of her assumed knowledge, deemed tawdry because of her associations, and judged because of her prior work as a stripper. Certainly she and, to a lesser extent, her daughter were the targets of a community's sympathy, shame, outrage, distrust, voyeurism, and guilt. With the scrutiny of the media focused on her home, Tina was someone from whom her neighbours would distance themselves. Even small talk was pained; however, if talk *with* her withered, talk *about* her escalated. With potentially justified assumptions that she was a serious drug user, there was little sympathy for her. She was written off as a "crackhead" and her young daughter pitied as a "poor kid."

Local residents wanted Tina and people like her to just go away. As in Shedden, they wanted peace restored to Iona Station; they wanted the talk at the Holland House to return to baseball scores and crops. They wanted the media and police to go away so they could just have a pint and a plate of fish and chips again, the way it used to be.

But the media and the police weren't going anywhere. This was too big a story, the biggest execution-style murder in Canada's history. The day after the bodies were discovered, the *London Free Press* offered a six-page spread with the headline "MASSACRE" displayed boldly on the front page. The CBC aired a clip of the Holland House and described it as a motorcycle-gang hangout, but Marty felt they edited his words so that he seemed to agree bikers were bad news. Eventually those charged in the murders were portrayed as heartless rebels with no regard for human life.

But beneath the headlines, beyond the sound bites, and between the reports, there are always stories that don't get told.

CHAPTER 4

Noblesse Oblige

> Time shall unfold what plighted cunning
> hides.
>
> —*King Lear*, act 1, scene 1

In Shakespearian tragedy, there are, simplistically, two ways to fall: the stars have crossed you or the feudal dimension of obligation wherein you are bound by oath and duty has gone awry.

Noblesse oblige implies that vassals must serve god and the king, but that the king must conduct himself nobly (deserving of service) and with charity to others. And in the feudalistic society, patriarchy rules, so the obligation also demands that sons must serve their father and women must obey all men.

It would seem that men on motorcycles are very unlike white knights on steeds, and the women who choose this company in contemporary society far from ladylike. But scratch the surface and the commonalities appear. Men and women alike vie for the affections of those they perceive in power. Respect must be earned to have duty bound.

If there is one firm code in the world of motorcycle clubs, it is that you never implicate a brother for a crime or otherwise jeopardize your brothers (*compadres* in Bandido terms) let alone jeopardize those in positions of power. The common signature at the end of a Bandido e-mail is "love, loyalty, and respect" and the common conclusion for any live conversation with another member is "Love you, Bro." 1% Motorcycle Clubs, as they are known in outlaw motorcycle gang terminology, have highly organized systems, rules, and rites of passage—but brotherhood is paramount.

And yet what if need to protect yourself from danger becomes more important than the altruistic ideals of a brotherhood? What happens when a man must choose between his own life and the lives of his brothers? Despite the brethren code, many bikers eventually turn against each other out of some of the basest of human emotions: greed, envy, fear.

"The Life" of a 1%er, as the brotherhood is called, has many rules that require strict adherence, an oddity for an organization of people who have complete disregard for societal laws and norms; a 1%er, according to the written Bandido bylaws, is in fact someone who has "given up on society and politicians [sic] one-way rules." The Life is lived with no regard for the law or its enforcers and no regard for societal expectations. Even above blood relatives, commitment is to be first and foremost to the club. "All members are your brothers and your family," reads the Bandidos creed.

During the 1950s the American Motorcyclist Association said that 99% of bikers are law-abiding citizens. Bike aficionados then came to identify themselves as either motorcycle enthusiasts or the self-defined members of outlaw subcultures (in other words, the 1% of motorcyclists who are badasses) who vehemently reject society and authority and define their membership with either three or five patches on their backs. The types of patches depend on a member's rank in the organization. Those deemed Friends and Hangarounds do not wear patches. "Colours," another term for the patches, have to be earned, and they are respected above all else. They are never washed because this would symbolize an attempt to erase one's history.

The biggest 1% organizations in the world, also called outlaw gangs, include the big four: the Hells Angels, the Pagans, the Outlaws, and the Bandidos. The Hells Angels and the Bandidos have always been full-out enemies around the world, but when various governments and police forces started coming down very heavily on these organizations in the 1990s and the 2000s, a sort of a pact was needed. It didn't mean there would be no fights and efforts to kill each other; it just wouldn't happen on a large scale anymore.

Once a man has joined a 1% organization, there are two ways out. "Out in Good" means he has left the club in good graces, welcome to return if he so chooses. "Out in Bad" is the equivalent of excommunication. That said, in some 1%er gangs the claim is that the only two ways out are "in good" or dead.

In the Bandidos' world, a full-patch member has five patches on the back of his leather vest, all blazoned red on golden yellow backgrounds (the colours of the U.S. Marines) and valued above any other possessions. The top patch (the "rocker") reads Bandidos. The middle patch is a large figure of a man who looks remarkably like the old Frito-Lay "Frito Bandito," but is actually referred to as the "Fat Mexican," a man with a beard and burgeoning belly holding a pistol in one hand, a sword in the other, and donning a large, yellow sombrero. Odd that their insignia is something of a cartoon character since all other 1% bike gangs choose rather violent

symbols. The bottom rocker would be the country of affilia-
tion, or, in the case of a probationary member, would simply
read "probationary." On either side of the Fat Mexican are
two diamond-shaped small patches, one reading "1%" and the
other "MC," an abbreviation for motorcycle club. Patches are
specifically placed and purchased only through the appropriate
channels (i.e., the international headquarters) at exorbitant
rates. In the case of the Bandidos, the headquarters is in Texas
and the international leaders all reside here.

There are many other rules for 1%ers. They cannot "wear
colours in a cage," meaning they aren't allowed to wear their
vests when inside a vehicle since cars represent the society they
admonish. They must attend mandatory "runs," the journeys
taken on various occasions in bike formation. They must
attend weekly meetings called "churches" and face severe
fines if they miss these. Missing only a few may mean that the
member faces demotion within the organization while missing a brother's funeral brings the most serious of penalties. As
with certain religions, excommunication is always possible; in
motorcycle clubs, it's called a patch-pulling.

One of the other key rules for becoming a Bandido, as
with the Hells Angels, is that you cannot become a member
if you have even applied at some point in your life to be a
police officer. If the member ever was a cop, or had even simply
applied for police service, and his brothers found out, death
would be swift and certain.

Despite popular culture's profile of bikers as fast and
free, 1% bikers reside in an extremely hierarchical system of
totalitarianism. Despite irreverence for political regimes, one
could easily imagine Mussolini or Hitler at the head of such
an organization.

According to one of the testimonies in court, Bandido
international president, Jeff Pike, put it this way: "If I tell

someone to go piss in a corner, he better go piss in a corner." If he doesn't, he's dead or out of the club. And there is a saying in the world of bikers that you are more likely to die at the hands of a brother you wronged than by the hands of your enemy.

In the Bandidos organization, the hangaround is the lowest level. He's not even a biker. He's just some guy who the real members let hang with the club. Eric Niessen, Frank Mather, and Brett Gardiner were considered hangarounds even though the prosecution would eventually try to prove Mather and Gardiner otherwise. The hangaround can be trusted, and if he has any ambitions to move into the organization, he is the grunt worker expected not to just "go piss in the corner" but to mop it up if someone did.

The prospect ranks higher than the hangaround, but is the lowest of the actual members. He typically does all the cooking, cleaning, beer runs for parties, staying up all night, and serving any menial task ordered by a full-patch member. It is a demoralizing position and the assigned tasks could be anything from cleaning up vomit to committing offences full-patch members would not want to have associated with them. But in order for anyone to move up in status, they had to "do their time" in this countercultural version of the fresh-man's existence. It was one of the basic tenets of becoming a Bandido and the official club rules lay this out explicitly in capital letters preceded by an asterisk.

*"DO YOUR TIME!"

The next level up from the prospect is the probationary member, a position that doesn't exist in the U.S. Bandidos club, but does in the European and Canadian organizations. Finally, the highest rung is the full-patch member. The probationary patch is then replaced with the country name. In order to achieve the position, the wannabe's mentor nominates him and all chapter members have to approve unanimously.

Or so the rules go. In Canada, though, a lot of the rules were taken with a grain of salt, if not a pound, and it would eventually jeopardize the organization nationally.

In all 1% clubs, each chapter has its own president, vice-president, secretary-treasurer, sergeant-at-arms, and road captain in the officers' club. Each nation has the same executive overseeing all activities of the various chapters, but the absolute power lies with the international executive. The sergeant-at-arms is the guy who serves up any punishment warranted. If a brother missed too many churches, for instance, the sergeant-at-arms was the one who would punch him in the head (or worse, depending on the infraction). The road captain is the one who organizes the regular bike runs. He's the tourism expert who determines the itinerary and accommodations. The secretary-treasurer is responsible for collecting the substantial dues and ensuring that a cut is sent to the national and international offices.

Outlaw gangs also get to have other vassals who serve them, called puppet clubs. These are clubs that aren't quite ready for the big time but support the chapters by paying dues and watching the backs of the outlaw gang. For the outlaw gangs, the money always flows to the top, and there is always a cut of the action, which could be pretty substantial if there are enough puppet clubs doing enough front-line drug running, pimping, and theft.

It probably goes without saying that women don't rank in this world. If a brother "checked out" another brother's woman (always possessed and objectified, but also protected once they had earned the right to be "the old lady"), he would be appropriately dealt with by the sergeant-at-arms. But if she wasn't owned? She easily faced any number of incidents all the way from physical assault to a full-on gang rape. It is dangerous business to be a woman hanging around such an organization without an immediate protector.

But if a woman has the love of a biker, she and her children will be protected from any harm whatsoever. The biker is the ultimate provider for the family. For some women, it is worth the chances one needs to take to live in such a culture.

Women are never permitted to be around for church, but they are welcome to parties and runs.

• • •

Some bike gangs aren't quite as perverse as others when it comes to the entertainment of the opposite sex. In Canada, most of the Bandidos had loyal partners and so the parties at Wayne's and elsewhere often were more like family gatherings than the stereotypical drunk-fest and gang-bang. The Hells Angels typically run things a little more according to old-school misogyny. The parties tend to be a little wilder and the drinking and affiliated "incidents" are more severe. This is an organization that takes itself deadly seriously, so the membership both works hard and plays hard.

The Hells Angels club has a murky history, in large part because, as in all 1% clubs, its members are sworn to secrecy and can only discuss club business with other (full-patch) club members. Still some have infiltrated the organization and written about both its history in violence and its currency in drugs. The club is variously: a group of self-described motorcycle enthusiasts who merely organize themselves for social events, and idealized as modern-day, free-spirited legends; and denounced by both the Criminal Intelligence Service Canada (CISC) and the U.S. Federal Bureau of Investigation (FBI) as a highly methodical, violent, criminal organization.

In Quebec, where the Canadian Hells Angels were founded in the 1970s, another emerging outlaw motorcycle club, the Rock Machine, was its key rival, and the infamous "biker wars" that began in 1994 and continued until 2002 would summarily take more than 150 lives, including innocent bystanders. The Rock Machine rose originally as a group of independent drug traffickers and organized crime families who didn't wear colours and could only be identified by their jewellery. But street-level drug sales have serious money attached; they eventually banded together and started wearing blue and silver crests with the common triplet of patches worn only by 1% clubs on their backs. The Rock Machine was suddenly a force the Hells Angels were forced to reckon with to protect their turf and the whole concept of 1% gangs, and the Quebec wars became a free-for-all series of bombings and drive-by shootings.

Maurice "Mom" Boucher was the leader of the Quebec Nomad component. The Nomads are the most elite group of Hells Angels members, and they carry out the most dangerous jobs with great precision, the equivalent of an American police force's Special Weapons and Tactics team (SWAT), or the Ontario police force's equivalent, the Tactical Rescue Unit (TRU). They aren't tied to a particular chapter, but selected from various chapters if they exhibit a certain skill set that makes them deserving of their status.

Authorities still are unaware of an elite group in the Bandidos, but there is some evidence that they exist—elusive as ghosts.

While the Outlaws, affiliates of the Bandidos, were able to keep the Hells Angels at bay in Ontario for some time, the 1990s would see various patch-overs (the burning of one organization's patches and adoption of the new club's) and allegiances established with other independent clubs. Soon the Hells Angels dominated in Ontario. Their rise was partially attributed to the practice of handing out patches to individuals, many of whom had not even achieved full-patch status in their own organizations. So while the Hells Angels presence grew, so did the number of informants working inside the club, and so did the club's vulnerability to major stings and massive arrests.

Just as when any business grows too quickly, there are going to be some major challenges.

The Bandidos organized out of Texas in part because of the refusal of the Hells Angels to allow Hispanic membership; one of the reasons the Bandidos symbol is referred to as the "Fat Mexican" stems from the Hells Angels' historic and endemic racism.

Formed in 1966 in San Antonio, Texas, the organization's gold and scarlet colours were modelled on the U.S. Marine Corps' motif, even picking up on some of the same sentiments, especially the phrase: "Kill'em all. Let God sort'em out." The club quickly grew to become the largest outlaw motorcycle organization in the southern United States.

The Bandidos had apparently not been as successful in establishing itself in Canada, but when the Outlaws patched-over to the Bandidos, the Hells Angels again faced a powerful adversary. As the slogan for the Bandidos, "We are the people your parents warned you about," the Bandidos were not just a threat to parents and children, but to the Hells Angels' established trafficking grounds.

However, the biker wars in Quebec had brought a wrath upon all 1% biker clubs, with police forces committing significant resources across Canada to take down as many bikers as possible. Though on less-than-friendly terms, a truce needed to be assumed to ensure that everyone could continue business as usual. But the other issue now arising as a result of numerous informants and major arrests was a seeping feeling of distrust among all brothers in any 1% organization. The brotherhood faced a huge chasm in which those tender human "failures" of greed, envy, and fear could fester.

Wayne was evidence of the fear factor. Over the years his paranoia reached an all-time high. He thought everyone was out to get him. He cut down most of the trees between his home and the Aberdeen Line, erected the barbed wire fence, installed surveillance devices, bought the Dobermans, acquired more guns and bullets, and walked the perimeter of his property with a gun just about every night.

He might have had reason for his paranoia, but it only fuelled further distrust by his Bandidos brothers. Wayne had always been crazy in a violent way. Now he was becoming unpredictable, a disposition that might put his brothers' lives at risk.

Those brothers were the Toronto-affiliated Bandidos members. Slowly but surely, their respect waned. Eventually they didn't even invite Wayne to churches and parties. Not one of them had the stones to face Wayne and try to pull his patch, but he surely was being excommunicated in the old-fashioned way of shunning.

Wayne was the national sergeant-at-arms. His brothers were breaking rules in doing this. But by this time, there was a lot of rule-breaking going on.

•   •   •

Wayne's history with bike gangs was legendary. He originally wanted to be a member of the Hells Angels, but they didn't deem him suitable material. His ego was bruised since he considered himself a genuine badass capable of anything.

"Fuck you!" was Wayne's response and he summarily went about the business of setting up his own outlaw gang that would have nothing to do with the Hells Angels. There were a few occasions where an HA member would take a run at Wayne with a gun, but Wayne was a feisty and wily guy who they could never take down. There were a lot of patch-overs and eventually Wayne found himself running with a group that would become the Toronto chapter of the Bandidos. A big "fuck you" to the Hells Angels from Wayne.

Eventually the Toronto group attracted a few new players. A guy named John Muscedere, who considered himself a boxing expert, came under Wayne's wing. "Boxer," as he came to be known, was not your typical biker. He came from an Italian family who ran a meeting hall in the Italian community of Woodbridge, just outside of Toronto, where police know a number of senior Mafia members live. Muscedere wasn't a Mafia member, but he had all the makings of the television character Tony Soprano: a good Catholic boy who went to church on a regular basis and took care of and pride in his family. Woodbridge also was home to a number of strip clubs where bikers hung out, and more than a handful of shootings had occurred over the years among the rival factions.

Muscedere certainly wasn't as crazy as Kellestine, but he eventually looked the part. He had piercing brown eyes and regularly wore a somewhat demented smile: Grinch-like, crooked and malevolent. Half the time he looked stoned, even if he wasn't. He was a great protege and Kellestine would teach him all there was to know about being a badass biker. Their friendship grew and most would say they became best friends. Kellestine brought Muscedere into the fold and supported him all the way up in the ranks to a full-patch member. Within a short time, Muscedere became the president of the Bandidos Toronto chapter.

Kellestine's aspirations were greater. He wanted to be the president of all Canadian chapters and the two men spent many a night trying to figure out how to start more chapters across the country. There were a few opportunities in Saskatchewan, Alberta, and British Columbia. Muscedere began hooking up with some of the "independent" members in these provinces as Wayne worked to re-establish connections with other biker organizations to encourage them to join up with the Bandidos.

The expansion had limited success. It seems some of the guys were not nearly as entrepreneurial, optimistic, or driven. Most of them were content to just keep it local and hang on to their little piece of the drug-running and prostitution revenues. They were a source of irritation for Kellestine. He called them lazy asses who shouldn't be able to call themselves bikers, but he didn't typically say that to their faces, just behind their backs. And, of course, if you are a regular mud-slinger, even friends might wonder what you were saying and doing behind their backs.

Muscedere and Kellestine's friendship deteriorated a bit. It seems Muscedere had found a new best friend: Luis Raposo, another Torontonian of Italian heritage. Raposo earned the name "Porkchop" because he had a substantial mid-section and wasn't particularly well respected by the other bikers. But Muscedere brought him along just as Wayne had fostered him.

Eventually "Porkchop" earned the moniker "Chopper." He had worked to get his body in top-notch condition and shed the extra weight. Cleaned up, Raposo looked like a Mediterranean runway model for fine Italian suits. He had strikingly handsome and masculine facial features and carried himself proudly despite the fact that he really hadn't had any successes in his life. And despite the long, dark wavy hair and the sex appeal of a Don Juan, Raposo didn't clean up. In fact, he regularly screwed up. He cycled up and down the Bandidos hierarchy because he couldn't seem to follow even the most basic rules. He regularly had a layer of grime, his hair was unkempt, his goatee was crooked and his scowls were menacing.

Raposo was a cocaine addict.

Because Raposo was a fellow Italian, he and Muscedere shared a bond. As such, Muscedere thought that he could help Raposo through his addictions and to rise and maintain some stability within the Bandidos organization. He eventually made Raposo the chapter treasurer. It wasn't a particularly wise move to put a coke addict in charge of money; for good reason, Kellestine never trusted the guy. But then, there's an old saying that you hold your friends close and your enemies closer. Raposo got the big hug and the "Love you, Bro" from Kellestine, just like everyone else.

So Raposo was a regular at Wayne's parties, wearing a huge silver cross to perhaps ward off any evil spirits. Any time a photo was being taken, Raposo made a point of holding up his middle finger, one of many adorned with heavy, silver rings, most of which had Bandidos insignia though it's doubtful that he obtained these through the "legal" channels of purchasing them from headquarters.

And in typical fashion of a codependent, Muscedere always believed that he would be Raposo's saving grace from the evils of his addictions. He apparently didn't know or accept that the success rate for a friend helping an addict friend is virtually nil.

Kellestine meanwhile, tripping on crystal meth on a regular basis, took the position of the pot calling the kettle black. "Fucking loser," he would say behind Raposo's back. Muscedere didn't take too kindly to that. It wasn't long before Muscedere viewed Kellestine as *persona non grata* at the Toronto parties and churches. John Muscedere should have known better than to fuck with Wayne Kellestine.

CHAPTER 5

The Birth of a Prince

Striving to better, oft we mar what's well.

—*King Lear*, act 1, scene 4

Brett Gardiner was born in Calgary, Alberta, 1984, to Welsh immigrant parents, Joan and David Gardiner.

Joan arrived in Canada eight years prior. What started out as a family vacation with her parents and sister changed fairly swiftly to a new life. She asked David to join her once she decided she wanted to stay. It was 1976; a year filled with political conflict in Wales that resulted in the introduction of the Devolution Bill as tensions between central and regional governments in Britain heightened. Joan's family was relatively apolitical; they owned a fish-and-chip shop and focused on keeping their patrons stoked with deep-fried foods and soft drinks. Joan's fiancé, David, was one of the regular patrons, a striking young man who had worked in the mines since completing his elementary-school education, less interested in the fish than the find behind the counter.

Joan was a beacon with her rosy cheeks and dark, curly hair and a sturdy but feminine frame; her smile was broad, mischievous, and sincere. David was a handsome six-two with the build of a man who had worked as a labourer all his life, strong and roguishly attractive with a glint in his large, brown eyes and a smile that had warmed many a heart. When the two had met at the restaurant, there was no turning back on the tide of a relationship. David and Joan married in Calgary, a simple yet romantic ceremony with the traditional vows of commitment.

Joan took a job on a production line for a telephone company; it didn't take her long to prove her talents and she quickly worked her way up, eventually becoming a purchaser for an oil and gas company. David took to a journeyman's trade as a machinist, completing his apprenticeship after four years.

Eventually they had enough money saved to establish a home in the suburbs of Calgary: a modest but spacious four-level back-split in a middle-class neighbourhood not far from the Bow River. Here Joan and David awaited the arrival of their first child.

June 19, 1984, marked the arrival of Brett Oliver Gardiner, his middle name a doff to his Welsh grandmother, Olive. Not one to shy from challenges, it was also the day that Joan had a Mickey Mouse tattoo inked on her shoulder to mark the occasion. It seems full-on labour was not enough with which to contend and here was further evidence of a strong woman with a fondness for the Disney fantasy.

Joan and David were in their mid-twenties when Brett was born, youthful enough to meet the challenges of an infant, the wants of a precocious toddler, and the passion of a young boy, with the same Celtic, brown eyes and heart-warming smile as his parents. His early years were spent with his trucks and the icons of the late 20th century: his He-Man action figure and his set of Teenage Mutant Ninja Turtles. They raised him to feel confident and competent, and their young son demonstrated strength of character from his earliest ages as he stood up to authorities if he felt something was unjust, asserting logic with the finest mannerisms.

When Brett turned 4, baby sister Sara came onto the scene. Joan and David had the million-dollar family, one boy and one girl—handsome, dark-haired, and dark-eyed, Celtic beauties.

David marked the occasion with a highly stylized tattoo of a dragon on his right forearm with Joan's name engraved therein, in a suitable Celtic font. He had a second tattoo to mark the loves of his life: J, B & S—Joan, Brett, and Sara.

Brett began attending the local elementary school at the age of 5 along with the many children in his neighbourhood and the surrounding new suburban communities. He adjusted well to starting school, establishing many new friends.

But grade one was a far more daunting year. At just 6 years old, Brett's teacher would not tolerate his excitability and his willingness to speak his mind. Admittedly, he was never rude, but he was ostensibly righteous and likely had some unidentified learning disabilities regarding his ability to focus. The doctors advised the Gardiners to set him on a course of Ritalin, a drug that was all the rage for active boys in the early 1990s when the diagnosis for attention deficit hyperactivity disorder (ADHD) became commonplace, almost too commonplace to be considered legitimate by many who were beginning to distrust the influence of large pharmaceutical corporations on medical diagnoses.

Brett's parents suitably investigated the benefits and detriments of the drug and decided it was not the best solution for their son. The possible side effects were considerable: abdominal pain, nausea, dizziness, cardiac arrhythmia, angina, and headaches to name a few. Possible long-term threats included paranoia, drug dependence, and schizophrenia, none of which the Gardiners felt could be justified when their son was just struggling a bit in school and needed to keep busy. Instead they directed him toward activities that would focus him, such as a type of karate that David practised and all kinds of other special hands-on local activities for children.

On the parent-teacher night, he bounced down the hall ahead of his parents, pointing their attention to the various artwork on the walls of the hallways—showing them the water fountains, the boy's bathroom, the tile lines that you had to step over so that you didn't "break your mother's back," proud and excited to have his parents in his prime milieu. He rounded the corner near his classroom well ahead of his parents in his enthusiasm and was met by his teacher.

"Brett! What are you doing here?" in a critical tone of voice.

She was likely embarrassed when the Gardiners, quite shocked by the teacher's scolding, came around the same corner shortly after their son. "Oh," his teacher said far more quietly and politely, "Mr. and Mrs. Gardiner. I didn't know you were here."

Brett was an excitable boy, indeed. Like many boys, he preferred to play sports and build widgets than trace out the letters of the alphabet on a stencil. Math, it seemed, was particularly frustrating for him with all of its attention to logic and memorization and little room for creativity and activity. As it turned out, Brett had severe intellectual struggles with his memory that would not be identified until long after he had spent more than three years in jail as an adult.

Nobody seemed to realize the challenges that he faced, and rather than seek out a psycho-educational assessment, his grade-one teacher opted to fail him while the school administration supported the decision. Joan and David Gardiner were not even made aware that a psycho-educational assessment was possible. Of course, it wasn't the norm then.

Like so many parents, the Gardiners were beholden to a system that maintained authority in educational assessment and a medical system that sought to drug those who were deemed incapable of following orders. Though Brett was a mere 6 years of age, the powers that be labelled him "difficult."

Joan and David had considerable reservations and many questions about this decision, but the educators assured them that it was for Brett's own good. His relatively young sister was turning 1, starting to make all of the wonderful discoveries of a toddler that keep parents exhausted. Joan and David had only ever wanted the best for their children and they caved to the suggestions of the authorities.

"He was always a good boy," Joan recounted. "He was rambunctious but always very thoughtful of others. He has always cared deeply about how other people are feeling."

For several years, likely suffering the same taunts as any child who has failed first grade, Brett kept his feelings to himself and he ignored any negative comments directed his way, remaining surprisingly content with his lot in life. He always walked away from a fight if the rivals were focused on him, but if their cruelty was focused on other children, he quickly and assuredly rose to their defence. In grade four, a new girl moved into the school; she was obese and bullied by her classmates. After witnessing the insensitive teasing, Brett came home crying to his mother.

"How can kids be so mean, Mommy?" He begged for an explanation.

Joan didn't have an explanation, but she did have some advice.

"You have been given a big job, Brett. You need to take care of her. Do you think you can do that?"

He nodded through his tears and they hugged.

"Okay. But I don't like school, Mommy. I don't like those kids."

The next day, Brett made a point of spending any spare time he could with the girl, befriending her as the other children quickly learned to cease their taunting. The kids came to accept both and became friends.

Joan and David knew that they were raising a good son with a good moral compass.

Brett demonstrated similar tenderness with his little sister. Though he bestowed upon her the expected behaviour of any sibling knowing just the right trigger points for annoyance, he also became her protector early on. As young children they shared one of the bedrooms upstairs in the Gardiner home. Sara was frightened without a light on when she went to bed, but since Brett could not sleep with the light on, he found a way to comfort her. He would put on a heavy, acrylic sweater, rub his hand briskly over his head, and take the sweater off shedding spectacular static lightning through the room to Sara's delight. She could always sleep after that.

Not only was Brett what Sara would call "my big brother, the shining 'night,'" Brett also prided himself on teaching her to stand up for herself. On one occasion while playing with her dolls in the front yard of their home, a boy came along riding his bicycle. The unwitting boy stopped and stared at Sara, much to her chagrin and likely only because he found her somewhat curious as she played with her dolls. Brett watched from the bay window indoors as Sara proceeded to push the boy off of his bike.

"Get lost," she said defiantly as Brett watched on.

Then she dusted herself off and beamed back at him through the window with a wave of her hand as she returned to her dolls. The boy apparently got the message and took alternative bike routes after that.

"I knew right then that I had done everything right for Sara," Brett recounted later. "I knew that if I couldn't be there for her, she could take care of herself."

With his younger sister's fears about the dark and bullies allayed, and his own needs for privacy increasing with age, Brett moved into a bedroom in the basement. As siblings will, Brett and Sara continued to coexist as best friends and arch rivals. In one favourite game, Brett would blindfold his sister with a scarf then chase and whip her with a Japanese bamboo sword called a shinai used in the martial art of kendo that David practised.

"We laughed and laughed, but I never let her do it back to me," smiled Brett.

One of Brett's other preferred games was called "King," in which Brett would wrap himself in blankets and Sara would be required to do anything he asked; feeding him was the priority, but cleaning up his room was also one of the standard tasks. He was, after all, an older brother and took the appropriate pride and privileges such a position availed. The bond of siblings is a curious thing.

"When I think back," Brett laughed, "It was kind of mean, the stuff I did to her, but she seemed to like it!"

Sarah concurred. "It's funny that my favourite game with him was 'King.' But, it was always like he was there protecting me so I liked being able to take care of him."

•   •   •

In a thriving new suburban development, many families with young children had moved in. Brett played with the neighbourhood girls and boys for hours at a nearby park in the middle-class Calgary community, a broad and heavily forested area where the children could play the games children play. Cowboys and Indians. Cops and robbers. Games that have clearly delineated lines about who is "good" and who is "evil," even if based on stereotypes and stigma.

Even without his friends around, Brett preferred to spend time at the park learning its many secret paths, using his vivid imagination as a knight or a police officer or a pioneering adventurer roaming the undiscovered wilderness. He was King Arthur on a mighty steed, Don Johnson from *Miami Vice* (sans the white suit), fur trader Simon Fraser, and he was many other characters that grow out of a boy's imagination. The park was Brett's sanctuary throughout his childhood and well into his adolescence.

Many of Calgary's parks and neighbourhoods are built on lands that were previously gravel pits, with literally tonnes of aggregate extracted from these sites used in the construction of municipal infrastructures and residential residences. This park and its suburban neighbourhood where the Gardiners lived was built on just such a site, a combination of floodplain, escarpment, and upper plain. As gravel pits in the 1970s got deeper and the cost of extracting aggregate escalated, many companies partnered with local government to ensure the land was put to good use, redeveloped for suburban neighbourhoods. The once cavernous pits in the floodplains became new sites for suburban recreation as the waters flowed in from the Bow River to fill them.

In the centre of this forested park were a number of such small lakes that the locals refer to as lagoons. Young adolescents would swing into the waters from ropes and tires attached to the overhanging trees. Older teenagers merely looked on, smoking a cigarette and trying to look cool for whomever they thought might care. Brett whiled away the days fishing in the various lagoons, learning that he could catch the smaller perch in the shallowest lagoon to snag the largest fish in the deepest pond. He was especially excited when he felt the resiliency of a pike on the end of his line, a strong, agile, fighting fish often breaking the nylon line after lengthy bouts trying to bring them in. But the game was always catch-and-release since the mercury level was significantly high and Brett really didn't have any interest beyond the sport and sense of accomplishment.

"The biggest one I ever caught was a three-pounder that I called Hooker because of all of the old lures stuck in this fish," he recalled. "It was a fighter to get by all of those hooks without getting caught. I kind of wanted to be like that fish."

Not to miss an opportunity to restore some lure that he had lost on many other occasions, he gently removed each of the hooks and returned his prize to its depths. Hooker was likely relieved to have some of its piercings removed and Brett felt a sense of pride in taking care of his find.

"I was like the guy who takes the splinter out of the lion's paw," Brett smiled with his doe eyes. "I felt like everything was right in the world, you know?"

The Big Rock, a 12-foot-high remnant of the glaciers also sat in the park and was a favourite haunt for the suburban children and teenagers to climb atop and pass hours in idle conversation and considerable quiet, as evidenced by the carved initials and spray-painted missives.

Meanwhile, he and his family took regular vacations to Penticton with their tent trailer, to Joan's sister's cabin in the Rocky Mountain foothills, and to the Okanagan beach, their lives epitomizing a young, suburban, middle-class family.

Brett continued to grow in excess of his peers, gangly and awkward but surprisingly content. When a new elementary school opened substantially closer to his home, he began grade six. It was the last grade of elementary school. Brett was still a year behind his age group, and still struggling. Midway through grade six, the educators made a second, critical decision. Based solely on his size, they decided that he should be attending junior high school instead of elementary school. Though the Gardiners had serious reservations, school administrators convinced them again that it would be in the boy's best interest.

He began grade seven in December of that year—a new school midway through the year, with few friends in attendance, cliques already formed, and the advent of adolescence rearing its ugly, hormonal countenance. On the first day at his new school, one of the boys in his class taunted Brett with a plastic knife; it was the first time Brett ever punched someone, serving to both protect him (and others) from further bullying but also drawing him under the watchful eyes of the school administration that immediately put him into a "behavioural" class with many other young men who had struggled in school and had inadequate guidance.

Turning into a teenager is not easy for even those who have breezed through their childhoods and here was a boy who decided early on that he desired both respect and popularity despite the challenges he faced. Like so many emerging adolescents, the focus of school became socializing rather than academics. As a student labelled with a behavioural problem, the challenge of establishing both respect and popularity became tantamount as he alternately confronted and admitted to the expectations of his Welsh parents that he always present himself as polite and well mannered.

"One day," Joan reported. "I got this phone call from a teacher who thought Brett was being a smartass by saying good morning to her every day. I was baffled. Why would it be a problem that my son had manners? Why would they treat him this way because he was polite? I just told her that we raised our boy with manners."

Indeed Brett did have behavioural issues. He was easily bored and frustrated, could not remember simple tasks or information, and he appeared defiant as a result of trying to be popular. He was a typical adolescent boy learning to be a man and he had choices to make as he defined his new role. He said, "I didn't want to be known as 'the dumb kid.' I wanted everyone to like me. And all the kids did! I mean, the teachers didn't like me, but I didn't care about that, you know."

· · ·

Most teenagers survive these years despite their various challenges and, especially given the support of their family, emerge as law-abiding citizens. Brett chose a thornier route.

Brett and his best friend, Richard Callen, began to spend more time hanging around together and less time in school. They found a new place to hang out instead of Brett's suburban neighbourhood, a place that was way more fun than school, an area of Calgary known as Ogden and what most people in Brett's neighbourhood would refer to as the wrong side of the tracks.

Brett had his first sexual experience here at the tender age of 14. At 15 he took up with Chance Fortune, the daughter of a Hells Angel.

Meanwhile Joan and David had finally saved up for the trip of Joan's dreams: Disneyland. But perhaps the Mickey Mouse tattoo on Joan's shoulder was something of the fantasy of young idealists who do not understand the many challenges of having teenagers. David and Joan packed up the car with the kids and drove from Calgary to California for the family vacation they had always dreamed of taking, staying in one of the finest resorts and enjoying their time away from work and school.

Brett went to Disneyland for one day, but had, for a period of time, ditched the family for other, far less pedestrian activities. Missing his girlfriend back home, he had sequestered himself in the hotel room where he racked up a $600 long-distance phone bill.

Chance told Brett before he left that she wanted an "open relationship." That didn't go over well with Brett who always thought that if you are with a person, you are with them.

"I guess I was calling trying to convince her to stay with me, but, I felt like, you know, here I am hundreds of miles away and I can't do nothing.

"I think I was feeling pretty rotten about my life. I found some other kids my age who didn't want to be in Disneyland.

We hooked up and I did my first line of coke. I got pretty high and wound up having my first threesome here." Brett paused. "I felt awful about doing that to Chance."

Chance, as it turns out, had no issues with disloyalty and the couple never did get back together. But what she did offer during their brief stint together was some insight into the criminal subculture of motorcycle clubs. Some of the guys in Ogden seemed to like Brett and even trusted him to run drug money. It was a pretty good gig and provided him with some cash for his newly found drug of choice: marijuana. He loved the high; it made all his troubles go away.

But this wasn't the only side of Brett during these increasingly troubling times for him. He was also deeply involved in the Navy League's youth program, the Royal Canadian Sea Cadet Corp, proving himself very disciplined during his four years—learning leadership skills, participating in various citizenship initiatives, and honing his physical fitness. Here was a place where Brett emerged in the top of his class, eventually joining the Guard, the uppermost echelon in the organization. He devoted every Thursday night and every Saturday to his regiment, attending many ceremonies, demonstrating his naval knowledge, establishing leadership skills, but also learning about the use of arms that can be used for virtue or vice.

Leadership in the Sea Cadets, however, required work, something the increasingly sluggish lad rebuffed. On his 16th birthday his best friends, Rich and Mike, had bought him a mickey of vodka, which he consumed with typical naive adolescent fervour.

"Mike was this guy who had all his shit together. He had the highest marks in school. He was a good athlete. He never did anything wrong, but for some reason he liked hanging with me and Rich. Like, he was always trying to be our friend even though he didn't really fit in with us."

Drunk and fearless, he spent part of that evening danger-
ously hanging from the girders on a bridge that towered above
the Bow River; it could easily have been his end, but typical
of his age, Brett thought he was invincible.

"You know, I was pretty messed up, but I felt like Super-
man. Like nothing could hurt me."

It was at this time that Brett determined the Sea Cadets
were no longer something he wanted to pursue. Smoking
marijuana exacerbated his laziness, the normal laziness that
afflicts many teens much to their parents' chagrin, and the
Sea Cadets took away vital time for him to socialize with his
other acquaintances. School, meanwhile, became increasingly
difficult and even less rewarding as the reports continued to
come home that he simply didn't apply himself. Indeed. Why
bother?

With his new indomitable qualities, the boy who once
cried over the teasing of an obese girl adopted some far less
empathetic qualities. Although Mike was his lifelong ally, Brett
became far less a friend and far more a foe. Mike was always
on the receiving end of Brett and Rich's malevolence. Sometimes they would shoot a pellet gun at him. On another night
they stripped Mike naked and tied him up on a cross for the
night. The sun was up before they released him and returned
his clothing. On yet another occasion, Brett convinced Mike
that if Mike held his hand down on the picnic table that was
their regular haunt in the park, Brett could fire a staple gun
such that the staples would go on either side of Mike's fingers.
Such was not the case.

Only once did Mike ever retaliate on one night of aggressive drinking, menacingly swinging an axe and threatening
that he was going to chop off Brett's arms. Thinking it a feeble
effort to demonstrate his bravado, when Brett extended his
arm on the picnic table and provoked his friend to cut it off,
Mike swung down in violent revenge.

"I was really lucky that I was fast enough. I never thought Mike would do something like that. It was like he went crazy for a minute."

As Brett reflected on his friend, a sadness overcame him.

"I brought him down," Brett would eventually say, shaking his head. "He wound up failing and turning to drugs. I think it was my fault."

With only a year and a half of high school under Brett's belt, increasingly absent from school, and only 8 credits completed of a requisite 100, he and Rich decided it was time to resign their academic efforts. However, on the day that the two young men made an appointment with the principal's office to officially terminate their secondary-school educations, they happened upon some marijuana and wound up missing their meeting. The next day Brett received a call at home that he had been expelled.

•   •   •

Brett's substance abuse gradually increased as he began experimenting with drugs other than marijuana, using cocaine, ecstasy, and acid with increasing frequency. These were all readily available provided one had the cash. Brett described himself as "lazy" and since he didn't have a job (even his gig as a drug mule for the bikers in Ogden dried up) he started stealing, selling off some of the family's possessions, and conducting various other scams that provided him his perks. It was about this time that his new-found friends in Ogden began to call him "Bull," a nickname that made the previously lanky boy especially proud. His other moniker was "Beau," reflecting his generous brown eyes and gentleman's smile; he had become a handsome and compelling young man.

While Brett and Rich were basking in their new-found life of leisure, Joan and David were becoming increasingly worried about their son. His new girlfriend, Heather, liked to see him dressed in expensive Ivy League clothing, button-down shirts and a sweater around the neck coordinated with classic pants. Since he had no income, he'd steal it, and she served as his "eyes." As the petty theft increased, so too did the heavy drinking and marijuana use.

On one occasion Brett had gone to pick up Heather at IKEA where she was working as a cashier part-time. Arriving extremely drunk, Brett made a decision to head to the nearby mall while he waited for her to finish her shift. He walked into one of the dollar stores and began pocketing a few items; he next went to a golf store where he snagged a bag. He continued his inebriated wanderings with utter foolishness, picking up various items in various stores and putting them into his stolen bag. By the time he staggered out of the mall, he had a wide assortment of nonsensical objects in his possession: a tool kit, some cans of Beefaroni, a package of toothpicks, even a pair of women's pantyhose. Beefaroni and a pair of pantyhose?

A steady arm secured his shoulder as he stumbled out the doors. "I'd like you to come with me, young man."

"I can't believe how stupid I was," Brett reflected with a laugh.

This was to be Brett's first criminal charge, less an act of crime and more an act of sheer idiocy.

Although certainly disapproving of their son's behaviour, the Gardiners continued to take care of their son and his less-than-stellar girlfriend, who was now living in their house. Parents never stop loving their children no matter how often a child may disappoint.

During their time together, what amounted to less than a year, Heather introduced Brett to the fine art of bank fraud. While working in her other part-time position as a bank teller, she would often come home with a few hundred dollars tucked somewhere in her most personal clothing, sometimes several times a week. She had devised a way to take money out of fictitious accounts providing the couple with a more lucrative lifestyle than could be expected while one was unemployed and the other merely working part-time.

Though certainly not rich, they had achieved a certain level of comfort and leisure that even allowed them to take a short vacation in the Rocky Mountain foothills about two hours outside of Calgary. David had driven them out to a remote campsite and deposited them where the couple drank, smoked pot, communed with nature, made out, and munched to their heart's content. Rich was supposed to provide their return fare.

After a week of rest, relaxation, and considerable partying, the food supplies all gone, what little money they had brought spent, and no sign of Rich, an alternate plan was in order. They decided that they would try to hitchhike to nearby Sundry, where Brett's aunt had a cabin and where he knew many of the local youth, having spent many summers here. It was about a 30-minute drive from their campsite and most of that they wound up doing on foot, amounting to several hours of walking the hilly terrain.

When they finally reached Sundry, they found a bank machine. Armed with expertise and a bankcard, they withdrew $800 from a non-existent account, all captured on security videotape and providing for their $100 cab fare to return to Calgary. Of course Brett thought nothing of the theft at the time, since his girlfriend had clearly proven this a successful way to get some extra cash and he himself did not conduct the bank fraud. Easy money after a difficult journey.

Shortly after, Brett celebrated his 18th birthday at the Duke, the local British pub where his parents regularly had a pint on Friday evenings. His parents had reserved the basement for his party, inviting all of his friends, both the ones they approved of and the ones they held suspect. After all, their child was becoming a man and he needed to make decisions about his own life. It was here that he met his next girlfriend, Abby, who was one of the servers at the event, and though she was currently involved with an abusive young man, Brett decided that he would work to win her affections. Abby's stepfather had contacts with the Rebels Motorcycle Club, a 1% club affiliated with the Hells Angels, and provided Brett opportunities to collect monies for the organization. Again, Brett had a job he could do and felt excited doing, and he had won over Abby.

Unlike his previous girlfriends, Abby liked being in the somewhat seedy hood and never asked Brett questions about his potential criminal activities. She grew up in Ogden and was comfortable with her background and the limitations of living a working-class existence within an environment where drug dealing and prostitution were the norm, where about 20 per cent of the population was deemed "low income," and where more than 35 per cent of the homes were short-term rental properties.

Heather never liked it there. She was into the "preppy" scene. So as Abby came aboard, Heather moved on. Brett never thought anything of their breakup because "we were so different." Brett just assumed Heather felt the same and didn't want to continue the relationship.

Abby's primary goal was having fun and life with Brett certainly availed this; however, it didn't come easily or safely. A short drive from Calgary there is a gorge where the cliffs, 6, 12, and 30 feet up, offer exciting opportunities to jump down into the cold mountain runoff—the kind of excitement Brett and Abby craved. However, rumours swirled about a death that resulted from a jump from the highest cliff point, so the couple and their friends limited their jumping to the two lower points, extracting their bodies from the icy waters and basking on the rocks amid the laughter and camaraderie of other Calgary adolescents. Afterward, Abby and Brett spent many evenings sitting around a bonfire on the cliff with other young adults, smoking pot and drinking cheap beer. These were the halcyon days.

Drugs played a central role in Brett's life and he rarely went a day without at least smoking some pot. On one evening around the bonfire by the cliffs, Brett and his friends swallowed copious amounts of ecstasy, a psychotic stimulant that has both the pleasant effect of increased energy with side effects of substantial paranoia and anxiety. When the Royal Canadian Mounted Police (RCMP) arrived in the area, clearly not as attuned to the many trails and tracks through the mountainous area, the teenagers scattered into the dense brush and made their ways back to their vehicles. Brett and his friends somehow drove back to Calgary, all the while consuming more ecstasy, so much so that Brett's tongue became so badly chewed that it is scarred to this day. They continued in their druggy fog well into the night, with Brett unsure of how he wound up in his own bed at some point the following morning when his family was out grocery shopping, and uncertain of how he had left a trail of garbage, dirty dishes, and cigarette ashes in his wake.

At this point, Brett was a jobless high-school dropout too lazy to even do the few chores around the house. His parents asked him to earn his keep, but he had refused to get up in the morning to go and look for work. His father had provided significant leads for him, at one point even lined up a job, but Brett didn't show up for the urine analysis that would have indicated what he was really up to in his substantial spare time. His parents were understandably losing patience with him. Sara, now 14 and having always been sheltered and cared for by her older brother, cried regularly about his decline into some questionable behaviours.

"I don't know what happened to him. He suddenly changed."

Brett knew it. He was a bad influence on his sister and he wanted to distance himself from her.

"She was doing all the things right. I was doing all the things wrong. I sort of feel like I was still protecting her by showing her all the bad stuff so that she wouldn't do what I did."

On this particular day when the three returned from their shopping jaunt, David became highly agitated that his son had, yet again, left the house in utter disaster. He had not raised his son to be such an indolent punk with complete disregard for family and society, but he also did not as yet know that his son was in his basement room sleeping off the previous night's serious intoxication.

As his father descended the stairs he was met with the further chaos of his son's sloth. Empty bottles were strewn about the room, a bag of chips was scattered on the floor, and cigarette butts were snuffed out in pop cans. With each step closer to his son's bedroom, David's temper rose. He woke Brett with a jolting yell and a push to his shoulder. David, of course, did not know that Brett was now entering the withdrawal phase of a druggy night with all of its symptoms of cognitive impairment, anxiety, irritability, and violent mood swings from depression to rage. A heated exchange of words followed, the television was smashed, punches were thrown, and then David retreated. Joan was standing in the kitchen crying as David mounted the stairs from the basement.

Sara retreated upstairs to her bedroom where she rocked herself in a fetal position amid despairing sobs. She had only recently entered puberty herself with all of its confusion and hormonal mysteries. What on earth was happening to "my big brother, the shining 'night'"?

Joan tried to calm herself by putting groceries away, cleaning the kitchen, doing anything to keep her mind and hands occupied, putting the milk in the cupboard and the cutlery in the fridge. David paced outside up and down the driveway. His body was still heaving and shaking, his heart racing, his head pounding as he stared at the ground alternately shaking his head and bringing his hands to his temples as he fought back tears.

With some force of decision he returned to the house and proceeded back down the stairs. Again there was a heated exchange.

According to his parents, it was the only time Brett was ever violent.

CHAPTER 6

The Unmade Minotaur

The gods are just, and of our pleasant
   vices
Make instruments to plague us.

—*King Lear*, act 5, scene 3

At 18, Brett had ironically earned the reputation of the bully he really never wanted to be. While he never sought out violence, he had always stood his ground if anyone dared to hurt someone he cared for. He was the brother who ensured Sara would be safe and never make the same mistakes that were presently leading him to a sad existence. He perceived himself as becoming the young man who brought misery into the family on a regular basis. No longer the son and brother named Brett, he saw himself as "Bull" with all of the word's connotations—the male who could not be controlled and the dung that he left in his wake. Over in Ogden, Bull became his moniker.

Even if his parents had forgiven him, Brett felt certain he needed to leave his family home and strike out on his own in order to prevent them any more problems with his life choices.

His feelings were further exacerbated when, on one particular summer day, he met up outside of the local liquor store with someone he knew and disliked immensely, a fellow Brett knew to have broken into his own house. But Brett was an opportunist. The tall and thin young man with a crooked smile and discoloured, rotting teeth was in possession of the one thing that could make Brett forget about grudges.

"I didn't like this guy. I knew he was trouble, but I wanted to get high and he had some pot. I loved smoking pot, you know? So we went to the Devonian Gardens in the mall."

The mall was the TD Square, an expansive shopping and financial centre in the heart of Calgary that also boasted a 2.5 acre indoor botanical park, fully climate controlled and encased in glass.

"We went in there and found a bench under some trees. It's a really cool place, this forest inside a mall. So we smoked a joint here and then got hungry."

When Brett and his new-found buddy finished their recreational adventure in the park, they sauntered over to the food court where Brett intimidated an A&W fast food attendant to give them free food. It was one of Brett's regular scams.

"I came in here an hour ago, ordered food, took it home and it was fucking cold!" He badgered the young man in his brown and orange uniform. "And it wasn't even the right fucking order!"

The attendant responded nervously under the glare of the neon lighting, apologizing profusely and saying that he would give them a free order now, to which the buddy piped in with his grotesque grin. "Yeah."

As they devoured their burgers and fries in their marijuana-induced "munchies" phase, a fire alarm resounded through the mall. As other patrons hurriedly left, the boys were enjoying the mellowing effects of the marijuana and in no mood to hurry out, snickering at the customers clutching their parcels and children as they rushed to the exits. When they were satiated, they meandered through the now cavernous hallways of the mall where they stumbled upon a Shoppers Drug Mart store and pharmacy that had miraculously been left wide open.

"It was cool being stoned and just walking through this big mall with nobody else in there."

Opportunity knocked first for Brett with a chance to get stoned and yet again with a chance to pocket some stuff.

They wandered through the store picking up items that might have some resale value, such as jewellery, cosmetics, and expensive over-the-counter drugs. The pharmacy itself was locked tight, so pharmaceuticals did not provide them any options, but by the time they were leaving the mall, Brett's buddy had a duffle bag full of goodies. Brett prided himself on being clever enough not to be the one holding the bag, so to speak. The only stolen property he kept was a package of Listerine mint-flavoured quick-dissolving strips.

As luck would have it, however, the score of the day was for the police officers waiting outside. It seems they had been monitoring the young men's behaviour once security cameras picked them up smoking pot in Devonian Gardens. When the two men exited the mall, they were met by four uniformed officers who admitted to being the ones to trigger the fire alarm and leave Shoppers Drug Mart unlocked, just to see what the two miscreants might do. The hapless two just stared at each other in disbelief.

The great Shoppers Drug Mart heist marked Brett's only night in jail. Shortly after, former girlfriend Heather—the one with a knack for theft and bank fraud—decided to take out her feelings of rejection and the need for revenge. Heather went to the police to tell them about the $800 bank-machine theft some time ago in Sundry. Her image had been "blocked out of the surveillance video," perhaps because she had by now paid back the money she had stolen and admitted her guilt in exchange for a shot at "the more serious criminal."

With these thefts under his belt, Brett now had a full-fledged criminal record. Too lazy to go to court when ordered to appear (since it would require him to get out of bed early and take a bus), warrants for his arrest, despite his only ever participating in petty theft, began to stockpile. The year was 2004.

"I went to my first Bandido party in Edmonton. I saw this guy with a big Bandidos charm on a chain and I knew I wanted one of those."

Though Brett didn't know it at the time, that guy was none other than John "Boxer" Muscedere. Muscedere was in town working to implement Wayne's ideals for expansion.

At this time, Brett was still trying to make something of himself in the "real world." He had registered in the Hilltop Security Academy's Calgary branch where he hoped that he might have a chance in a career as a security officer. However, when the Hilltop Security Academy had finally fully processed Brett's background check and discovered he had a criminal record, the pursuit of this goal was dashed.

But the background check took many months, enough time for Brett to establish a relationship with "the love of [his] life," Regan M.

"At first I thought he was just a jerk," Regan said. "But I grew to fall in love with him. He always went out of his way to take care of me."

He wrote her poetry, he made her feel happy when she was feeling blue, and he made her believe in herself the way no one else had.

• • •

For someone who is equal parts indolent and disenfranchised, options for income are limited; one such option was to help move drugs, and a local 1%er who called himself "Preacher" offered Brett just such an opportunity. Preacher was then a member of the Pilgrims, a Christian motorcycle club with three missions:

1. an evangelistic ministry meeting together for the purpose of spreading the good news of eternal life through Jesus Christ to other bikers;

2. providing fellowships with other Christian motorcyclists working to bring unity to the body of believers in Jesus Christ, and;

3. providing an environment that encourages new and young believers to grow in their faith, while watching God work in their lives and the lives of other members.

Christian motorcycle clubs are remarkably well populated, but Preacher had a strong interest in bringing the gospel to the non-denominational 1% bike clubs with the motto "We pray for 1%ers." He saw himself as the conflation of Billy Graham and biker, mounting his sermons in bars instead of a pulpit.

As part of his mission, he baptized Brett as a born-again Christian and he exposed his new disciple to many bike clubs in his efforts to bring Jesus into their houses and hearts. Preacher was a compelling character, articulate, thoughtful, and clearly value-oriented, but he was also someone who tended to be attacked on a regular basis by the non-believers.

Together Brett and Preacher travelled to Prince Albert, Saskatchewan, where the Hells Angels had a puppet club called the Freewheelers. In order to establish any status, even as a hangaround, Brett would have to put in long hours serving full-patch members, on one occasion bartending from 6 p.m. to 5 a.m. at a club function. Evangelizing proved to be exhausting work, and Preacher did not see a bright future in his conversion efforts in Prince Albert. Perhaps he needed to move to more promising territory.

The Preacher's next effort was in Toronto with a motorcycle club known as the Loners. It was a club founded in the late 1970s in Ontario and included a chapter near London led by none other than Wayne Kellestine, a brief stint for him between his work with the Annihilators and the Bandidos. The club was, of course, a rival of the Hells Angels.

Brett devotedly followed Preacher to Ontario where he got a security job at a strip club, which presented many opportunities for Brett to engage in activities with the strippers; but he was not interested. His heart was back in Calgary where Regan was expecting his child. He worked six days a week at the Club Pro in Woodbridge and lived for free in a house in Brampton, a Toronto suburb that was then a cheap alternative to high city rents for many new immigrants; it is also infamously inhabited by many gangs.

In addition to meeting some of the Loners at Club Pro, Brett was introduced to the evolving Toronto Bandidos chapter members as well, though he would not get to know any of them very well. The club would eventually be subject to many police raids. In December 2006 tensions between the Hells Angels and the Bandidos came to a head, resulting in the fatal shooting of Hells Angel David "Dred" Buchanan by Bandido Frank Lenti. According to the newspaper reports, Lenti was working the club's security at the time of the shooting. He was charged with second-degree murder despite reports in the newspapers that police believed there was a contract out on his life. Eventually the newspapers would report that Carlo Verrelli, another Hells Angels member who had been fired upon that night, was suing the strip club for $1.1 million for psychological and physical damages.

However, in 2004, it was a safe haven; so safe, in fact, that the cast of *The Sopranos* had come to Woodbridge to study their characters via the Mafia and 1% clubs. The television show centred on the lives of an Italian organized crime syndicate in New Jersey. Woodbridge was not only Loner territory, it was also home to many members of Toronto's Italian organized crime syndicates. Though Brett determined that he was not a good son back home, he thought he might prove himself as somewhat successful from a distance. While serving his long hours at the club, Brett also met the actors and had them autograph a book on *The Sopranos*, which he shipped back to his parents who were fans of the show.

Some months passed while Brett worked security for the strip club in the forsaken suburbs of Toronto and Preacher mounted his sermons to the boys on bikes. Brett gave up drugs, except for the occasional joint. He was intending to turn his life around.

Preacher was not as charismatic as he may have needed to be, however, and the Toronto Loners weren't exactly taking Jesus into their hearts. The preacher decided that he and his ministerial disciple should return to the prairies, to the town of Odessa, just outside of Regina, Saskatchewan. Here Brett found employment working in a liquor store that also operated as a bar and tattoo parlour—one-stop shopping for sailors had there been a port nearby instead of the spans of wheat fields. While he did not make much in terms of an income, he had an opportunity to adorn himself with many tattoos.

On his right arm, he had a tribal symbol inscribed in addition to a tattoo called "Alice in Hell," which vaguely resembles the original John Tenniel illustration of a young girl with long, blond locks and a frock that served as the visual backdrop to Lewis Carroll's celebrated work. This Alice, however, was covered in blood and wore an expression of horror. On his left forearm, Bull selected another somewhat disturbing image, something akin to an alien holding a bloodied axe, maybe a remake of *The Flintstones* cartoon character The Great Gazoo gone mad.

There were other far less gruesome and far tenderer decorations, as well. Over his heart he had his girlfriend's name tattooed, then the love of his life, who he thought would be his angel through thick and thin. On his right arm, in a Celtic font, he had the name of his as yet unborn son Evan inked into his skin.

Brett also had one more tattoo that he wouldn't be able to divulge to others. It was the Bandidos logo over his right chest. It was a dangerous thing to do since he was not a member and bikers who found out about it would surely have had issues with his use of their property. But then, Brett was cocky and naive.

• • •

Meanwhile, Preacher deemed himself a pastor deserving of his own flock, so when the Hells Angels puppet club the Freewheelers discovered that he had been in conversation with arch-rivals the Bandidos and the Loners back in Toronto, they told him to pack his bags and bibles and take the next coach out of town. A few serious beatings confirmed his need to leave. It was June 2005 and Brett decided he had spent enough time following Preacher around Canada. After all, the wanderings had proven neither as lucrative nor admirable as originally promised. In all of his adventures he had established no affiliations with any motorcycle clubs and wasn't even committed at this time to becoming a 1%er. Moreover, he couldn't join even if he wanted to since he wasn't the requisite 21 years old.

In turn, Brett moved back to Calgary and began to live with his girlfriend Regan and her mother. He then got a job in Medicine Hat, in southeast Alberta, close to the badlands, a slightly rolling prairie area that locals call "The Hat" about a three-hour drive down Highway 1 out of Calgary. The born-again Christian was determined to alter his life, make amends to his family, and become a responsible husband and father. His friend Rich joined him at his place of employment and they embarked on an effort to become sheet metal workers. The income was far from stellar and the men with whom he worked didn't exactly fuel his self-esteem, but there was some stability for him after his nomadic efforts to become important.

He celebrated his 21st birthday back in Calgary with his parents and his now-uncomfortably pregnant girlfriend; it was the marker of his manhood with all of the responsibilities he was now was prepared to face: No more drugs. No more wandering. No more trying to be an important guy. Just be a good dad and partner.

Shortly after his birthday in late June 2005, a series of treacherous storms struck southern Alberta. Three severe storms left rivers bursting their banks, damaging 1 in 10 homes in Calgary and causing 14 municipalities to declare states of emergency. Perhaps most seriously hit was the Okotoks area just south of the city.

Rich's father, Rick Petrie lived along the Sheep River in a rundown Okotoks residential campground that suffered particularly sudden and devastating flooding. Rich's brother, Steve, lived with him. They were run-of-the-mill poor guys living in an old trailer in Lion Park. On June 29, Rick and Steve decided that they should support the rescue efforts in the park, and so drove a backhoe out into the river to help mend banks and secure land, helping people whose scant belongings had washed down in the river's current. The rain fell hard and thick around them as the muddy waters rushed over the backhoe. But something went terribly wrong when the backhoe became grounded in the thick mud; a wave came up and washed the father and son off the machine. Steve made it to shore. Rick vanished.

At his residence in Calgary, Rich received the phone call from Steve about their father's disappearance. Distressed, Rich still took the time to drive the several hours to Medicine Hat to help Brett get to work, and from there proceeded back north and west to the Okatoks campground to help in the search for his father. Within a half hour of his depositing his friend at the sheet metal shop, however, Brett received a call from Regan that their baby was being born. Rich rushed back to take the new father to the hospital in Calgary. It was July 2 when Evan came into the world. Rich's father, meanwhile, had been missing for three days.

Rescue efforts at the Okotoks campground were meagre. A handful of volunteers, none younger than 50, were undertaking the search; one was heard to whisper that Rich's father was "just a dirty old biker." No other official rescue efforts had been established. So, on July 3, just a day after Brett's son's arrival, Rich drove into Calgary to pick up his friend so that they could both join in the search efforts. Exhausted from the long drives, long days, and a long labour, they spoke little on their journey here.

When they arrived, they had to park quite a ways from the park itself. They came upon the park office, which had been almost submerged, vending machines tossed aside, the colourful playground equipment thick in sludge, swollen waters still rushing under the bridge carrying felled trees, white sandbags close to the shores where the rich people lived.

The two stepped carefully through the dense brush along the swollen river. Inside of 20 minutes, they found what they had feared as Rich stood dumbstruck for a moment and then collapsed to his knees into the muddy bank. Just five feet from the body were other footprints; how had that rescue volunteer missed the man on the shore?

"Rich and I were so fucking mad. How could they leave rescue efforts to a bunch of old people and not bring in some other help? Where were the cops? Where was the army?

Where was help?" Brett later recounted. "Nobody cared about
him because they thought he was just an old, poor biker. They
didn't know him. They didn't care."

Brett grabbed his friend by the shoulders and yelled to
him to go for help. Rich, shocked and confused, nodded and
ran down the path back to the volunteer station.

Rick's head was oddly propped up on some branches of
a birch tree, but the bulk of his torso was buried in the dense
silt. From what Brett could see of the body, it was distended
and the arms twisted about in caricature as if some poorly
produced movie dummy from a 1940s film had long been left
behind on a movie set. He began to dig frantically with his
hands through the thick silt and in the drizzling rain.

"I didn't know what to do. I just knew I had to get him out."

The volunteer team came by shortly before Rich's return,
trying to console Brett as he concentrated all of his energies,
holding back his fear and rage. At one point, one of the volunteers thought it reasonable to dig with a shovel and Brett
pushed the man over just as he was preparing to bring the
shovel down.

"What the fuck are you doing?" Brett yelled at the volunteer. "You're gonna chop off his legs!"

Shortly after, a police team arrived and they brought
Rick out of the mud and strapped him to a board. Brett was
distraught but, as with many people who find themselves in a
moment of tragic peril, he did what was necessary to help the
body escape this mucky, makeshift grave. By now, Rich was
returning to the brush; he, Brett, and the police officers carried
the board back to where the coroner would eventually arrive.

As Brett tried to console his friend, they each opened a can
of Lucky Lager beer, Rick's favourite, and poured the liquid
into the river—keep wake to the wake. They then each took a
twig from the tree that had somehow reached out and pulled
Rich's father from the river and stood on the bank staring out

into the waters. Without a word, they laid their sticks down as a cross on the ground and stood arm-in-arm in silence.

Years later Brett would learn that the birch tree is affiliated with the medieval rune that resembled a *B*, symbolizing rebirth. But right now, it was just an effort to come to terms with a devastating loss.

The media arrived within minutes of the discovery of Rick's body, setting their cameras on both the muddied bank and the two 21-year-old men walking arm-in-arm on the pathway. Brett was infuriated by the intrusion; he scowled at the cameraman and told him to fuck off as he tried to shield his friend.

"I couldn't believe they would do this. How can you just come in and take pictures of people when they've just gone through something like this?" Brett paused in retelling the scene. "I just wanted to punch the camera guy."

"They didn't care that Rich's dad just died an awful death. They just want to leech off other people's misery," Brett sighed.

A still caption of this video footage would eventually become the only photograph of Brett ever displayed in the media during the Bandidos murder trial, and the picture would never tell the thousand words of new life and tragic death that these two men had just faced during the early July days of 2005.

"Now they put this picture up to show me as a monster. Just a guy who tells people off. They don't care now about telling the real story behind that picture."

CHAPTER 7

Ambitions and Assemblies

> The art of our necessities is strange,
> That can make vile things precious.
>
> —*King Lear*, act 3, scene 2

Clearly Wayne Kellestine and John Muscedere had similar aspirations originally. They had wanted to see an expansion of the Bandidos across Canada. At some point, however, Muscedere's ambitions waned. He was more interested in his own local chapter and his evolving friendship with Luis Raposo. Maybe Muscedere just wanted to focus on getting Raposo off the drugs, and it seems Muscedere no longer had the same respect he once had for his mentor. Kellestine was pushed to the periphery, left off the guest list for parties. Kellestine knew that the only way he could resume any stature would be by getting another club started.

There were some other problems arising in Toronto. Most of the guys didn't have bikes, an absolute prerequisite for being a biker. With Raposo as treasurer and coke addict, Toronto dues were not reaching head office, and head office was starting to get a little ticked with the Canadian boys.

Wayne wanted to restore order, but he knew the Toronto brothers weren't going to let him start his own faction in London, so he had to go broader afield. There were a few guys in Winnipeg who might just do the trick if Wayne could convince his Toronto brothers to sponsor them. It was going to be a hard sell.

One of the guys in Winnipeg approached the Toronto boys on a few occasions. Michael Sandham was a little guy, standing a squat five-three with a chubby cherubic face, shorn hair with male-pattern baldness setting in. He didn't look like a biker, but he was a smooth talker and owned a Harley.

Wayne liked him well enough, and after the Toronto men met Sandham a few times, they agreed to consider taking him into their fold as long as Wayne did a background check and the guy turned out to be okay.

Either because of physical similarities to the pudgy yet predatory, skunk-like carnivorous Australian marsupial or to the Loony Toons character (neither of which is particularly attractive), Sandham's "biker handle" was "Taz." Despite his small stature, he had a compelling ability to sell people on his ideas and make people believe he was important. He was articulate and keen to demonstrate himself as somebody deserving of a following, presenting himself as an expert in weaponry, biker culture, and the allure necessary of attracting international affection from the Bandidos organization. The Toronto bikers perceived him as that stereotypical used-car salesman who they weren't sure could be trusted in the pitch he delivered or the hog he rode in on. But Sandham could charm snakes out of trees and weeds out of woods.

And Wayne was hungry for a new pack. So despite the standard requirement for a background check in the biker world that is even often more sophisticated than the checks police conduct, Wayne somehow didn't do his homework.

Wayne had ambitions. Sandham had dreams. The little guy from Winnipeg had not been able to make much of a success of himself. He trained in the military for a bit, but lacked the courage to become a soldier. If he couldn't be a soldier, he thought he might be able to establish some sense of prestige in another career that many who want power pursue. He thought he could become a police officer.

He first joined as an auxiliary member, basically a volunteer giving out parking tickets. He then joined a small force just outside of Winnipeg, but it seems his colleagues didn't give him the respect he thought he deserved. So he came up with another plan. He would be a badass biker.

Now there is a code in the biker world that anyone who was a police officer, in fact, anyone who had even *applied* to be a police officer at any point in his life and tries to join a bike gang, is worse than a cop. If the bikers find out, his life would be worth less than dirt.

So Sandham had to play his cards right if he were going to be successful in this pursuit. His first effort was with the Ontario-based Outlaws club. As he tried to straddle both being a police officer and a wannabe biker, he submitted a letter to his supervising inspector that he was attending a family funeral. He was subsequently caught on surveillance spending a full week at an Outlaws clubhouse in Sault Ste. Marie at the time of an Outlaws member's funeral. He resigned his position with the police force when he faced an internal review for lying about this association. The Outlaws, a club in Ontario affiliated with the Bandidos, would similarly dismiss him from any chance of entry because they learned he had been a police officer. Sandham was faced with a quandary.

He saw the Toronto Bandidos as his next option, befriending Wayne Kellestine at several parties. Had Wayne done the
homework with which he was charged by the Toronto chapter,
Sandham would likely have wound up like O'Neil, the cop
killer found behind Wayne's place with three shots to the head
that stuck out of a shallow grave.

Even though the Toronto Bandidos had not approved
Sandham for membership yet, Sandham returned to Winnipeg
from one of the churches on a mission to recruit. Ironically,
Sandham only knew about bike gangs because he had read
about them on the Internet. That wasn't what he would tell
the folks in Winnipeg who he sought to recruit.

A fellow named Ron Burling with long-standing connections to several biker organizations was the first Sandham
approached. Ron is a muscular guy, six foot two with his head
shaved, a dozen tattoos, and a menacing goatee, a good guy
to sidle up to, Sandham thought. Burling's picture appeared
on a website that identified all the dangerous folks in the
biker world. So word on-line, on the street, and in the press
about Burling was that he was a super-badass affiliated with
the Hells Angels. Best not tell him the story about being a
Bandido member. Instead, wait and see how things pan out
with the rival club.

Burling was a full-patch member of a club called the
Redliners, a puppet club of the Hells Angels. He seemed to
think highly enough of Sandham to introduce him to a friend,
a guy who can only be identified as MH, because he is now
under witness protection.

Growing up in Winnipeg, Manitoba, MH had never
travelled farther outside of the city. He struggled for his entire
life with medical problems and learning difficulties and MH
eventually wound up on welfare while Burling introduced
him to the lucrative life of dealing drugs. Though apparently

not intelligent or healthy enough to find or keep work, MH thought he still had the street smarts that would keep him safe in a dangerous game. Two to three thousand dollars a day selling cocaine at a Hells Angels bar known simply as the Zoo supplemented his welfare cheque and helped him provide for his wife, children, and ailing mother. Though initially working only with Burling, profits would skyrocket once they began working with the Redliners. Sandham saw Burling as an "in" to the culture and didn't seem to care which team he joined.

MH was not a 1%er. He wasn't deemed to be good enough by the Hells Angels or even the puppet Redliners club, but they would let him work for them because he could do the dirty work of dealing at floor level—selling individual packets of coke rather than moving large quantities. It is the easiest place to get busted and members, even probationary ones, don't want to do a job where they are likely to be caught—and this is where MH was arrested for trafficking in 1999. Over the two years of his dealing, MH reported that he earned more than a million dollars tax-free; under what had become a heavily policed welfare system, he would not have been able to purchase any goods or property that would tip off the government about his additional earnings. And yet, by the time of his sentencing for trafficking in 2002, only two and a half years from the time of his arrest, he claimed he had spent it all. On what, he couldn't recall. (Or did he even get the money he was owed?) Perhaps prophetically, MH didn't even buy a motorcycle. Or perhaps when the witness-protection program wells dry up, he will have a stockpile somewhere waiting for him to carry him through the rest of his life.

It wasn't until after his arrest that he would undergo a series of psychological tests to determine the extent of his disabilities. At the time of his pre-sentencing hearing for trafficking, MH's lawyer made submissions on behalf of medical reports that he had a grade-5 reading level with an impairment in intellectual abilities such that he could not even gain, let alone retain, employment. The submitted psychological testing identified severe cognitive constraints showing that his range of abilities, given his age and education, could be considered a severe disability. It was no wonder that he dropped out of school by grade 11. He was an adolescent with some serious memory and mental health issues.

During the two years between his arrest and his sentencing, MH worked at a local pool hall known to be a frequent haunt for the Hells Angels and became a hangaround when the Redliners disbanded, and another club known as Los Bravos patched over to the Angels. In the realm of 1% motorcycle clubs, affiliations are always changing and monopolies on turf are frequently a source of tension.

Without a motorcycle, MH could not climb the ranks in the Hells Angels beyond the levels of hangaround, though he did manage to ascend from their lowest rank of "friend." Meanwhile, MH became a hangaround at another Hells Angels haunt.

Bumpers, the pool hall and peeler bar in Winnipeg's seedier part of town, was certainly not a gentleman's billiards club. The tables were well worn, the liquor was fast and flowing, fights were frequent, and the women were cheap. Cash was easily dispensed from wads of bills stored in men's black leather vests and sex workers easily found cocaine. One would be hard pressed to find a man here without tattoos and bravado, or a woman who had not spread her legs for a bit of pain relief.

Bumpers was also one of the meeting places for all ranks of the Hells Angels: friends, hangarounds, prospects, full-patch members, and even officers.

Aerial photo of the Shedden Massacre dumpsite including the Steele's home.

Russell and Mary Steele leave the courthouse after testifying to the findings near their farm.

Aerial view of the Kellestine enclosure, complete with swastika behind the barn.

Police cruisers parked outside Kellestine's home.

Kellestine home after a fire destroyed it in Spring 2009.

"Big Pauly" Sinopoli in the hatchback.

Pallbearers entering the service for John Muscedere.

Jackets of the Winnipeg men. Sandham had the Canada rocker while Aravena had the probationary rocker—not official property of the Bandidos as the patches were made locally.

Michael Sandham is led in shackles to a plane in Winnipeg.
(WINNIPEG FREE PRESS/JOE BRYKSA)

Marcello Aravena is led in shackles to a Winnipeg plane destined for London.
(WINNIPEG FREE PRESS/JOE BRYKSA)

Lead Crown attorney, Kevin Gowdey, reads a statement to reporters following the conviction of the eight men.

Christopher Hicks speaks to the media after the convictions. Though Mr. Gardiner fired him, he attended court in the gallery as a show of support to his client.

The first sign erected at the site was removed. A second sign was erected with more nails; half of the second sign was pulled off.

The cross erected by the Kriarakis family near the site of the findings. It no longer remains.

Brett Gardiner, 2011

(Courtesy of the author)

MH, with his large and threatening appearance and dopey willingness to follow orders regardless of the risk, claimed that despite his low status in this highly militaristic operation he served as security for some of the highest ranking Hells Angels on several occasions during their visits to Winnipeg and Bumpers. Maurice "Mom" Boucher and Walter "Nurget" Stadnick were legends in the Canadian history of bike gangs. While socializing with Nurget and guarding Mom, this was also the time MH first met the individual he would eventually call his brother in the Bandidos and best friend in all else.

Dwight Mushey, a confident, intelligent, and regal-looking man of Iranian and Philippine descent, was attractive to MH. Mushey was smart enough to invest wisely and had the stealth to keep law enforcement completely oblivious to his activities. Standing over six feet tall, with a slender but athletic build, long, dark hair typically neatly pulled back in a ponytail, and refined, wire-rimmed glasses, he commanded respect. As a martial arts expert with a black belt in tae kwon do, he had the striking combination of spiritual demeanour and combative precision. MH, prematurely balding, with a stocky body and certainly less-than-promising future, looked up to Dwight and felt honoured when he acknowledged him, a puppy wanting desperately to be taken seriously by any top dog. Why Dwight would take an interest in MH was an ill-fated mystery. But then Dwight was always a giver and always took care of underdogs.

Dwight's keen abilities to earn and invest had enabled him to purchase a large house in the relatively upscale Winnipeg neighbourhood of River Heights, even though his home was in the less desirable area close to the railroad tracks. As well, he had become a part owner in Phat Daddy's Restaurant, a bar frequented by many Hells Angels, investing in the establishment with former Winnipeg Blue Bomber lineman turned boxing promoter, Eddie "Earthquake" Blake, who now referred to himself as "Phat Cat."

Through his drug dealing and working at Bumpers, MH had established himself in Winnipeg's criminal subculture, earning the trust of some less-than-legitimate businessmen. MH had reportedly met Dwight while chauffeuring Phat Cat in his black Cadillac limousine from which Eddie liked to be seen stepping out, flanked by scantily clad young women. Dwight, or "D" as he became known, was an exceptional businessman who didn't care for the flair. He had other ambitions.

Over the next couple of years, the relationship between Mushey and MH became closer. Despite reports to welfare that MH had serious physical conditions that prevented him from working, he went to the gym regularly where he joined Mushey in bench-pressing and bicep curls. By all accounts, MH was still a fat guy, but he was bulking up. Mushey, on the other hand, was a strong, lean machine.

They hung out and played video games, drank beer, listened to Lynard Skynard, and planned their futures in Mushey's spacious home where D's sister, Sharon, also had come to live for a while. It seems that she had been physically abused by some guy she was living with so she needed a place to stay; the man was later found bludgeoned in a back alley. Nobody was ever charged for the crime and Sharon was left in peace.

MH and Mushey became best friends. You could be sure that one would cover the other's back when troubles arose. One significant problem arose for Mushey when he was charged with trafficking in illegal substances. As the local papers had it, he and Phat Cat had allegedly been moving ephedrine, a key ingredient in methamphetamine, from Thunder Bay, Ontario, to various black-market labs throughout Canada and the United States, and were now facing charges of conspiracy to produce meth. The way the police told it, there were strong connections with the Hells Angels and there was serious money to be made in meth.

It was late 2005 when Sandham came into the fold. Mushey, who was still awaiting trial for the alleged meth production conspiracy, didn't need to be found having anything to do with drugs or the Hells Angels.

But Sandham was adamant. "Bandidos aren't like the fucking HA. It's about the brotherhood, not about drugs."

In the old days, he would have been right. There was a little bit of dealing to keep money coming in, but it wasn't like the Hells Angels organization, which is far more dangerous, strategic, and lucrative. The Toronto Bandidos were a brotherhood. Its leader, Muscedere, was a good old boy who would tell prospects that it had nothing to do with making money. It was about the Friday nights being together in a testosterone-filled room where everyone felt the power of kinship. The AC/DC tunes would blare and the boys would feel like they were in a place where, no matter what, they had love and respect.

"Fuck the money. Fuck the drugs. Fuck the women. They aren't what's it all about. This is what it's all about," Muscedere would say thumping his fist against the left side of his chest. "It's about knowing who you are and being a true man."

Muscedere was a true man, true to his word. But Sandham didn't have Muscedere's presence. Mushey and MH were skeptical about this little, balding man with the squeaky voice trying to convince them that brotherhood is manhood. They weighed their decision carefully. Ultimately it came down to the fact that Ron Burling was the one to make the introductions. Burling was a real biker and would have (should have) known that Sandham was the real thing. Somehow Sandham snuck under his radar as well. Nobody knew Sandham had been a cop and he kept telling them that his connections in the biker world were broad and deep.

The thing is Sandham's story kept getting better the more he told it. Not only did he say he was in with the Toronto Bandidos as a prospect, but he reported that his brothers were asking him to start a new chapter and he would have the power to fast-track MH and Mushey through the organization.

Sandham was the man. Despite his small stature and high-pitched voice—antithetical to the embodiments of masculinity and bravado—he was a slick salesman. By December 2005, Mushey and MH agreed to join the fold. After all, they already had grown close enough to consider each other a brother. Why not join up with other men who also relished such friendship above all else?

At the time of this decision, Mushey's sister, Sharon, was out in her own place again, and Mushey's home had more than enough room to house someone else down on his luck.

Marcelo Aravena, despite his numerous losses in mixed-martial-arts matches and his reputation as a ne'er-do-well bully, was a security guard at Phat Daddy's before the big bust went down on the drug scandal and an ensuing sale of the restaurant. With more than 40 fights under his belt and only a handful of wins, Aravena earned his meagre living by being the guy everybody beat up in the ring in the evening, and then bullying drunken patrons late into the night. Not a life to be envied, but a steady income before the fall of Phat Daddy's.

Just as Dwight Mushey earned the moniker "D" coming into this burgeoning friendship, Aravena was given some biker handles, though substantially less flattering: "Fat Ass," "Mountain Gorilla," and the "Great White Chilean Ape," referencing his roots. His boxing name had been the more affirming "El Condor," but he was now in semi-retirement, presumably because he had suffered so many injuries that he had grown old far too quickly. Although a bully by nature, Aravena was a simple and sincere man. He did indeed resemble an ape with his bushy eyebrows, black, oval eyes, and his cranium shaped in a Darwinian nod to evolution. Though he spoke with the vocabulary of an 8-year-old, a strong speech impediment presented him as something more gorilla than human. His tongue struck his soft palate in a combination of some phonemic and phonetic disorder, so he likely needed to establish himself early in his life as a ruffian if only to dismantle stereotypical assumptions about a boy with a lisp.

In early 2006, Aravena was more down on his luck than usual; he was now struggling with a crack addiction and had sold off nearly all of his possessions to fuel it. His rent was long in arrears and he couldn't seem to see his way out.

Mushey was there for him giving him a room of his own and the support he needed to kick his habit.

Yet another young man packing problems without possessions would soon also land on Mushey's doorstep and come to count on his generosity. Brett Gardiner was hightailing it out of Alberta where Regan's mother had slapped him with a restraining order that prevented him from seeing his girlfriend and son. He didn't know why she suddenly hated him so much and he didn't have much choice but to avoid her. He arrived via some Bandidos connections in Saskatchewan and had been able to get a flight into Winnipeg where he heard a start-up Bandidos club was in the works. At the time he thought that if he could just make something of himself farther east he would be able to convince the loves of his life to join him.

Mushey and MH picked him up at the airport and took him to a bar where Aravena was working as a bouncer. Mushey "bought the house," meaning all of his friends could drink whatever they wanted, as much as they wanted, on his tab. Brett was suitably impressed even if his new-found friends were not particularly trusting of him. He seemed too young and impetuous. Mushey told Aravena to keep a close eye on him for the night.

They did keep an eye on Brett that night. Fortunately, nobody did anything stupid.

So the Winnipeg "gang" came to be, even if nobody other than Sandham had a bike and none of them had more than the potential for a patch. Heck, Aravena didn't even want anything to do with the organization and Brett was just looking for a ticket to ride somewhere cooler.

CHAPTER 8

Less Kin, Less Kind

Men must endure
Their going hence, even as their
   coming hither.

                        —King Lear, act 5, scene 2

MH had a little secret.

It all stemmed back to his trafficking charge when he was selling coke packets at the Zoo. His bust was a little unusual. He didn't actually have any coke in his hands at the time of his arrest. The stuff was upstairs in a hotel room being weighed and packaged by more established members of the Redliners. It was a typical day and he was just waiting for a guy to bring him the packets he was to sell that night.

He certainly didn't anticipate his arrest as he was just standing in the bar waiting for his delivery when a bunch of coke packets suddenly appeared on the floor. Or so MH tells it. His arresting officer was Police Constable Tim Dyack with the Winnipeg police. And Dyack didn't really want the low-level grunt worker. He was after bigger fish.

It didn't take long for MH to rat out one of those bigger fish: none other than Redliners/Hells Angel member Ron Burling. Perhaps Burling never knew that was the reason he was nabbed for trafficking. MH merely received two years' house arrest for his efforts. Burling was eventually going in for a lot longer and for many more serious crimes, eventually even one involving the kidnapping and torturing of a rival drug dealer in February 2005 that would see him spending eight years in prison.

During the two years of MH's house arrest from 2002 to 2004, he had one regular visitor who hung out with him. Eventually, MH referred to this man as Tim, no longer Officer Dyack. It seems Dyack knew MH was both well connected with the biker world and that it wouldn't take much to have him roll over on his brothers. MH came to count on Tim as a buddy, but, of course, he would never divulge this relationship to Burling, or to Dwight Mushey. It never even occurred to him that it might be a conflict of interest to be joining the Bandidos while serving as a police informant.

So it seems from its inception in 2005, the Winnipeg Bandidos were going to be facing some challenges. Sandham wanted to be the president of the chapter but there was a "former" member who Sandham wanted to oust. That guy, at least as Sandham reported, was doing drugs and wasn't good for the organization. That's why he needed a new set of boys to follow him and needed to make some better contacts than he had in Toronto. So here's the ex-cop wanting to take the helm; paranoid Kellestine almost 2,000 miles away being shunned by the Toronto chapter and wanting back in at an executive level; and MH, the police informant who wasn't quite bright enough to understand that's what he was. Mushey was the only one who wasn't playing anyone off each other; he was just trying to take care of friends. Mushey and MH had been fast-tracked by Sandham to become prospects, even though he didn't have the power to do so.

The fact that Mushey, MH, and Sandham were not actually accepted into the organization was evidenced in their patches. They didn't purchase them through the necessary channels and with the high fees attached to getting one's colours. Instead they had them made locally and got Aravena's mom to sew them on.

Meanwhile, the Toronto Bandidos were facing their own set of challenges. Dues weren't going to the U.S. headquarters and Toronto wasn't communicating with the mother ship. Texas was not impressed.

During the autumn of 2005, written contact among Winnipeg, Toronto, and Houston grew heated. Yet, as in all relationships coming to closure, there were more than subtle signs from far earlier that problems prevailed.

An e-mail dating back to fall 2004 from the Texas head-quarters perhaps spelled the first signs of an imminent decline. The U.S. Bandidos made an effort to interpret the issues in the aftermath of the 9/11 attacks that left border security more than reluctant to let anyone with criminal records cross.

Head office was trying to tackle the problem via e-mail.

"Seems like we have a problem here. You can't come here. We can't come there but you do not want to answer any questions. There are issues that need to be resolved. I've made attempts to get these answers but as yet I've not," came the message from Bill Sartele, the leader of the international organization, also referred to as El Presidente.

Cross-border resentment settled in among the Bandidos as a full year passed after Sartele's e-mail; some of the chief officers of the Texas headquarters were facing prison sentences and the international order reassembled itself under new leadership. Toronto and Winnipeg were not the gravest of concerns and the faltering communications were put on hold while the club dealt with bigger issues. Sartele was going to prison. A new president had to be put in place. The job would fall to former vice-president Jeff Pike.

Finally, in October 2005, an e-mail was sent from Texas to the Toronto chapter, written by the new El Presidente: "Canada has not been meeting the requirements of belonging to this club under the United States." Clearly the Toronto group needed to re-establish connections and pay dues, but they didn't seem to understand the seriousness of the situation and merely ignored the missive.

And then, just as the winter solstice was striking north of the border, the international Bandidos headquarters in Houston issued a clear directive to the Toronto group via Pike: "To Whom it May Concern: For the past year or more, we, B.M.C. U.S.A. have attempted to make communications with Canada. We have directed face-to-face visits for whoever is in charge up there. Up 'til now there has been no visit from the proper person. It has been decided that due to lack of participation, Canada's charter is being pulled. Effective immediately, return all Bandido patches and property."

Pike would eventually tell a CBC reporter that he had to do this. "I sent an e-mail—this was December or the beginning of January—and I cancelled all the charters in Canada," he said. "It was the only way I could get their attention. And I said, 'Well, if you guys don't want to be part of the club, if you don't want to communicate with the United States, then the hell with you and you go do something else.'"

If the order were obeyed, there would cease to be any Bandidos chapters in Canada given that Winnipeg was under the sponsorship of Toronto. Instead, Raposo insolently responded to Houston in another e-mail: "Being a Bandido in good standing is my world. Quite frankly I resent having to go through this. I've always done the nation proud. We've conducted ourselves as gentlemen and righteous brothers through and through. Never wavering, never in doubt that we were part of the best club in the world."

What the Toronto group perhaps misunderstood was the very hierarchical nature of the Bandidos nation as the Toronto members requested a worldwide vote from their brothers. The brotherhood is not a democracy, and this action raised the ire of the international centre even further. In the Bandidos nation, orders are given, not suggestions or requests, and Toronto was skating on very thin ice by refusing to follow the Texas missive.

Meanwhile, Sandham was desperate to save the Winnipeg club given his significant investment in it. The probationary chapter's "president," as he now deemed himself, decided that he needed to begin communications directly with the U.S. Bandidos, again stepping out of militaristic protocol by attempting to involve the international headquarters in local issues.

"Probationary Bandido Taz here from Manitoba Canada. I'm just hearing about a problem with Toronto. I hope that this [will] not reflect on us. We have worked very hard here for almost a year and a half. The day I became part of this family was a great honour for me and my crew. I hope that we can work together to remedy this situation." He provided his phone number in Winnipeg and the phone number for Kellestine over near London, signing off the e-mail, "Much loyalty, love and respect."

• • •

While Toronto members were seething, Sandham and Kellestine were scheming. They had managed to set up a meeting with some Washington State Bandidos via a former (excommunicated) Toronto brother, David "Concrete Dave" Weich, who now lived in Vancouver. Despite being out in bad with Toronto, Weich had been accepted for membership with the Washington State chapter. It appears they were effectively doing an end-run around Bandidos headquarters. The question remains whether the International/U.S. Bandidos were aware of the meeting.

Weich strongly resented the brothers who had pulled his patch years ago and was happy to hook up with Kellestine and Sandham. A fellow named Mongo, the international sergeant-at-arms and member of the Washington chapter, suggested the meeting.

With both American and Canadian members facing challenges crossing the border, an ideal location for a meeting presented itself in White Rock, British Columbia.

The Peace Arch Park straddles the Canada-U.S. border and offers a unique symbol of partnership between the countries. Dedicated in 1921 to commemorate a lasting peace, the park is managed by both B.C.'s system of provincial parks and the Washington State Parks and Recreation Commission. Since it sits astride the 49th parallel, it provided the possibility of a Bandidos meeting without either group crossing. On a cold day in March 2006 and under the flags of the two nations, Sandham and Kellestine met with their American counterparts. Kellestine and Sandham argued particularly effectively that Toronto members were not following the Bandidos laws regarding payments and performance; they left this meeting with the understanding that Kellestine was to be the national president of the Canadian Bandidos and Winnipeg would be the new Canadian chapter. In his new, as yet undisclosed, role, Kellestine was ordered, at minimum, to pull the patches of his Toronto brothers.

It isn't clear from the evidence, but the order may have been more significant: to kill Muscedere and another Toronto member, Frank "Bammer" Salerno. Salerno was hooked on heroin; sinking a hypodermic needle in your arm is a definite no-no for a biker.

A big question remained: Were Kellestine and Sandham ordered to kill? If so, did Bandidos headquarters order the hit?

Had Kellestine revealed his status and orders (whether it meant pulling patches or something more serious) to the Toronto group, they would most certainly have killed him, so all of his conversations with his Toronto brothers were to remain respectful and loving. While he likely salivated over the idea of being the one at the helm for the entire country, he was also astute enough to know that his assumption of the throne needed to be strategic. Indeed, the scene had all of the trappings of a Shakespearian tragedy.

When Toronto hosted the national Bandidos party on March 18, 2006, neither Kellestine nor any of the Winnipeg brothers were invited to attend—a significant snub.

Within two weeks of the Peace Arch meeting, Sandham received a phone call from his Vancouver connection. According to Sandham, Weich told him the orders were official: the Winnipeg members—MH, Sandham, and Mushey—were commanded to drive to Toronto to "take care of" Muscedere and Salerno. Why did Sandham get the call? Why didn't Kellestine since he was the one originally ordered? Why did Sandham feel he needed to call Mongo to confirm the order? Sandham reported that Weiche and Mongo were both pretty angry about that.

Perhaps the U.S. Bandidos had some reservations about Kellestine's frame of mind, or perhaps Sandham just had some delusions of grandeur and miscommunicated the missive so that he could seem the big man. Whichever was the case, the outcome was that no one was to advise Kellestine that they were coming to his farm, and that if Kellestine proved problematic, he was also to have his patch pulled. Good luck with that.

So Sandham loaded up his red Jimmy truck with the supplies they would need for the trek. If anyone knew of a planned murder at this point, it was only Sandham. He merely told Mushey and MH that they had to go down to Toronto to talk to the boys there, and maybe, just maybe *if* the guys wouldn't comply, pull their patches. Mushey in turn told Marcelo Aravena and Brett Gardiner that this was their chance to go meet the big guys to see whether they would be approved to come on board as prospect members.

Mushey asked Sandham if guns would be needed. Sandham assured him they would not.

Gardiner was elated at the prospect of finally being able to join a club, since he was now 21 and could formally be considered. Aravena just agreed to come along and still wasn't even sure he wanted to join. MH, of course, remained clueless, but knew that he was expected to go.

Kellestine may have known that head office had ordered the murders, but, at this point, all evidence suggests that he didn't even know the Winnipeg boys were coming to his place.

They headed out on Wednesday, March 25. Mushey rode shotgun while Sandham took the wheel and MH and Gardiner were relegated to the rear seats. Aravena had a "big fight" and so he agreed to fly down to London after his event. The drive from Winnipeg to London is a long haul at over 30 hours if you don't cross the U.S. border, and Sandham wasn't going to let anyone else drive.

With Gardiner as a mere hangaround in the vehicle, no Bandidos business could be discussed. Instead they made the two-day trek with the regular banter about music, the boring landscape of rocks and trees and more rocks and trees, and, of course, how great brotherhood is and could be, finding classic rock radio stations along the way.

Perhaps there was another reason for the Ontario journey that Sandham would not divulge to anyone. Perhaps the reason for the murders was far more complex than the Crown would later present as mere tensions among members within the same organization. It would be far more difficult to prosecute at an international level.

One theory suggests that a Toronto prospect, a fellow named Jamie Flanz, had stumbled upon a substantial stash of cocaine in a car deserted in a parking lot near Toronto while he was trying to eke out a living towing cars to pounds. A former biker infiltrator going by the name of Alex Kaine was hired to do some investigation by one of the defence teams and this was what he had discovered. The fallout of this theory was that the meeting at the Kellestine farm was set up in order to ensure a transfer of the cocaine, allegedly property of the Hells Angels, to a safe haven in another province. Or maybe, just maybe, Kellestine had made a deal with his arch rivals to either get the coke back in their hands or take care of the guys who had wronged them.

The Toronto Bandidos, after all, could not hide such a cache from such a skilled organization. If Sandham knew anything about such an opportunity for fortune, he certainly did not share it with any of his passengers on the trip down to London.

But the coke stash would only ever be a theory that nobody could (or wanted to) prove. It would, however, explain why Kellestine would eventually be the most brutal with Flanz. If Flanz did find a Hells Angels stash and not turn it over, there would be a serious price to pay for the whole Bandidos organization.

Dialogue was stilted for the more than 2,000-mile drive from Winnipeg to Kellestine's. Pulling patches is serious business and Sandham, MH, and Mushey didn't know what they would face when they arrived at Kellestine's house. Moreover, since Gardiner was only a hangaround, he was not privy to club business; indeed, he only knew Kellestine by reputation.

MH could never have known about the alleged find of cocaine or else he would have surely divulged this to his trusted buddy back home, Officer Tim Dyack. So, apparently, everyone kept their own secrets and ambitions to themselves on the long drive.

As the Winnipeg men got closer to the Kellestine farmhouse, they were not sure if they would be met with brotherly love or psychotic paranoia. Would their lives be at stake either at the hands of Wayne or the Toronto Bandidos?

To the delight of the Winnipeg members arriving at the Aberdeen Line farmhouse, Kellestine was highly receptive. They hugged, drank beer, and settled into various sleeping accommodations in the house, Sandham bedding in the recreation room behind the pool table and MH, as the largest man, taking one of the sizable couches in the main room. Once Aravena arrived from Winnipeg, he took over the other couch and Gardiner was relegated to the floor in front of the great stone fireplace. A few days after Aravena's arrival, Frank Mather showed up with his pregnant girlfriend in search of a room for a few nights while they sorted through their itinerary that had recently left them homeless. The couple established themselves on the makeshift bed in the cellar with the various rodents that scurried across them through the night.

For two weeks the men did virtually nothing. They watched pay-per-view movies on television, ventured over to the Holland House for fish and chips where Sandham picked up the tab, cruised to the nearby town of Dutton to use a pay phone, and, on a couple of occasions, drove the full 20 minutes to buy supplies of drinking water, toilet paper, and chips at the Wal-Mart just off the highway in London. They went to the nearby reserve to stock up on tree branches for a bonfire. They periodically met up with some of the local ne'er-do-wells, including a neighbour of Wayne's, an aged, former bank robber named Merv Breaton who had now turned to street-level trafficking of prescription drugs.

Breaton had a colourful history having served time for bank robberies throughout Canada and the United States, even serving time in the infamous Alcatraz prison and befriending the renowned Robert "Birdman" Stroud. But Breaton was now pretty much at the same point in his career as Kellestine—old, demented, and on the decline. He eventually told police that he was "born to be a fucking hooligan" and that the only reason he stopped robbing was because he "got too old to jump over the countertops." Breaton served up a bunch of rusty old bullets in a woolen cap as he asked Kellestine to "take care" of someone who owed him money.

There was also a visit to a fellow at the nearby reserve who was potentially going to give Kellestine some shingles. Though no one knew it at the time, it seems Kellestine had some weapons stashed in his roof and might need to do some "repairs" after all was said and done. Nobody knew why Kellestine wanted shingles. That was just Kellestine and you didn't ask.

They stole a trailer from the reserve, Sandham banging up his Jimmy in the process. It turns out it was full of frozen pizzas and the group would be eating well.

Nobody ever wore their colours; the Winnipeg men had decided to leave any vests and patches back home since Toronto would not have approved of their homemade attire that went against all the rules.

Mather had nothing to do with their jaunts and escapades as he preferred his girlfriend's company. Kellestine's wife Tina went to work while their young daughter, Kassie, caught the school bus every morning.

With virtually no running water at the farmhouse, the cluster of men was likely a scraggly and malodorous lot, not likely to have attracted much small talk with the locals.

There was a fair combination of camaraderie and contempt over those two weeks. Gardiner especially suffered the regular taunts. During one dinner, Kellestine told him to go outside and get some pickles from the pickle tree. As Gardiner went out in its search, his brothers laughed for a full 20 minutes before he returned frozen and empty-handed. When he reported that he couldn't find the pickle tree, Kellestine again sent him outside to look for it. Upon Gardiner's second return, Kellestine left the dining room and returned with three or four perfectly sliced pickles: "See. I told you it was out there."

Gardiner knew there was no such thing as a pickle tree, but he also knew that he was expected to be the butt of jokes since he wasn't even a prospect in the world of bikers he thought he might like to join.

That was only one of many times when Gardiner was ridiculed. Aravena was ridiculed, but not as much. Since they had absolutely no status in the club, Gardiner merely accepted the denigration as a necessary rite of passage, while Aravena merely took the abuse the same way that he had taken punches. Though a simpleton, he met every insult with self-assurance and the mistreatment merely rolled off of him.

During one of the men's visits to Dutton, MH slipped away from the others to call Dyack, but the police officer was on holidays so he left the message that he was at Kellestine's to pull Toronto patches.

On April 6, MH made a second detour to a phone booth while his buddies shopped. This time he reached Dyack. MH explained then that the Toronto members would be called to a church at Kellestine's farm the following day. There was nothing exciting about his phone call and certainly no hint that violence was waiting in the wings.

If MH thought murder was even being contemplated, he would surely have reported this.

On that same day, however, Sandham had made contact with Concrete Dave Weich, who had advised him that two Toronto Bandidos members had driven to Winnipeg to kill Sandham. When Sandham contacted his wife, she confirmed that three bikers visited his sister-in-law's house.

"Where's Taz? We've got some business with him."

Of course Sandham would be in defence mode once he heard that Bandidos were seeking him out back home. It seems that Kellestine had been in defence mode his entire life. And it was now reaching a fever pitch.

Kellestine and Sandham began to assemble for the worst as presumably the Toronto boys would not be happy to lose their patches. It might mean that the patches would have to be pulled under the threat of guns. Meanwhile Gardiner went about his duties at the farm: serving the members, washing the dishes, and hauling the water in from the well so that they could flush the toilet. Aravena mostly slept and watched television. Nothing different. He was always the lazy guy at Mushey's, so he was also the lazy guy at Kellestine's.

At one point during the two weeks, Kellestine uttered his favourite tough-guy Marines' sentiment: "Kill 'em all." Apparently he had forgotten the part about letting God sort them out. Though it was merely a macho mantra recited by a man who had likely read one too many *Soldier of Fortune* magazines, the Crown would eventually persuade the jurors that it was indicative of a plan to commit murder. Even though heavy-metal band Metallica's debut album *Kill 'Em All* went triple platinum, the Crown argued that the sentiment uttered by Kellestine was divorced of any affiliations to soldiers or rock groups. It seems the ironic nuances were missed. Instead, the focus of the statement was a literal translation.

At one point during the second week, Kellestine had donned a full army getup complete with camouflage war paints and had told Gardiner and Aravena that he was going to use a knife to slice up all the bodies after the church "and cook them up."

As they looked on with a combination of fear and horror, Kellestine laughed his guttural laugh, "I'm just fucking kidding. You guys take things so fucking seriously."

But Kellestine had a considerable stash of weapons strewn about his farmhouse, some that had clearly not fired for many years. He had old military items, mortar shells, German helmets, and even a garrotte, a type of torture device with two ringed wooden handles that had a ligature of piano wire strung between them. Apparently it was a device historically used for strangling a person, a rather strange souvenir, but then Kellestine was, if nothing else, decidedly eccentric.

Whether any of the guns would actually fire, especially if they were stoked with Breaton's rusty bullets, seemed unlikely. The Toronto Bandidos would not be met with a militia by any means. Presumably if there were really a plan for anyone to "kill 'em all," the boys would have at least tried out the weapons. And if there was really going to be a transfer of cocaine to the Winnipeg group, MH would have known about it and conveyed the information to his officer friend. Clearly, the only information Mushey and MH had was in regard to the simple act of patch pulling, with weapons present to ensure everything went as smoothly as possible, pretty much the norm in the biker world as a show of force rather than a threat of real violence, but that's a subtle distinction that most law-abiding citizens would not care to make.

• • •

On the afternoon of Friday, April 6, Kellestine, MH, and Sandham huddled inside and around a phone booth as Kellestine made the call to the Toronto officers with a message of the utmost urgency. While the Toronto members argued among themselves about the nature of the missive, many of them agreed this was a church requiring their attendance.

Kellestine told them that the Winnipeg guys would be at the farm later that night, after Kellestine had a chance to talk to his Toronto brothers.

"We need to sort this shit out," Kellestine told his brothers.

Meanwhile, Kellestine sent Tina, Kassie, and Mather's girlfriend away for the night. After all, women weren't allowed to be at churches.

The Winnipeg miscreants assembled at Kellestine's farm. Mushey attempted to saw off the barrel of a shotgun with a rusty hacksaw that afternoon. Sandham produced a number of pairs of surgical gloves from his duffle bag, gloves he had because he sometimes did tattooing on the side. He ordered the men to put them on.

As they donned the plastic gloves without really under-standing why they were doing it, Gardiner took some heat for repeatedly breaking his. Always the butt of criticism, he put on set after set and never asked questions.

Some of the men that night donned leather gloves on top of the thin plastic ones, in the case of Mushey, even affixing his gloves to his jacket with duct tape. The crown would eventu-ally argue that this "gloving up" was because they knew they were going to be killing. Who knew? Certainly not Gardiner, Aravena, and Mather. Certainly not MH and Mushey. They were just following what their leaders told them to do. It made sense to not want to leave DNA on any of Kellestine's weapons. After all, who knew what those guns were up to in the past?

Since they couldn't be part of a church and were just going to be sitting in the house, Mather, Gardiner, and Aravena eventually threw the latex gloves on the pool table and went about their business of watching television, drinking pop, eating chips, and smoking cigarettes. Another day in paradise. Gardiner and Aravena were just awaiting the day they would make the big trip to Toronto to meet the head honchos, and Mather was still trying to find an affordable place to live in or near London.

Even though Sandham and Kellestine spoke of "preparing for the worst," clearly this was not a group of men who knew what they were facing.

Kellestine was in his element as he prepared for the church, having likely consumed enough cheap beer and speed for the arrival of his Toronto brothers who would also reach their destination that April Friday night with an appropriate balance of cocaine, pot, heroin, and sobriety in their ranks.

It all begs the question: Why would the Toronto guys head to Kellestine's place instead of asking for a more neutral ground or meeting on their own turf? The answer was simple enough and it was the reason some of the guys who weren't coming tonight had gone to Winnipeg beforehand.

They knew Sandham had been a cop and he needed to be dealt with accordingly. Weapons packed for the job. They likely told Kellestine they were going to "deal with the pig." So Kellestine accordingly assured them that the Winnipeg boys wouldn't arrive until after the church. A little white lie.

CHAPTER 9

Exodus

I am tied to th' stake, and I must stand
the course.

—*King Lear*, act 3, scene 7

If the night of April 6 was party night, the morning of April 7, 2006, was spring cleaning day at the Kellestine farm.

There was a lot to clean up. A lot of evidence that would have to be destroyed. Keys, cellphones, a blood-splattered couch, and blood-soaked cash all had to be disposed of. Sandham may have had enough basic military training to know his weapons inside out, but apparently not enough to build a campfire, let alone a fire that could handle a couch. Someone figured out that they needed some gas for the job, maybe the gas that we would eventually find out wasn't available the previous night to fill the tank of one of the cars.

In the barn where the party had taken place, the floor needed cleaning. Kellestine had an old jug of muriatic acid, a cleaner strong enough to remove traces of blood.

Mushey, MH, Aravena, and Sandham helped for a while with the tidying, but were antsy to get back on the road and get the hell out of there. There was no room in the Jimmy for Gardiner. Maybe it was a distorted sense of loyalty that prevented him from fighting for a space. Maybe it was because he had always known that he was at the bottom of the pecking order, the butt of the biggest jokes. Aravena was thoughtful enough to give Brett all the money he had, 20 dollars. Mather had no vehicle so he had no choice.

As Mushey, Sandham, MH, and Aravena loaded their minimal belongings into the red truck and prepared for their departure, Kellestine gave Aravena an extra-big hug.

"You sure you don't wanna stay?" Kellestine sneered.

Aravena declined. "I gotta go take care of my mom. She's sick."

"Remember what I told you," Kellestine glared as he gave the fighter a "loving" smack to the back of his head.

Aravena merely nodded. He still didn't know if he was going to get out of there alive.

As they drove away, they spoke little and they didn't pull over until they were a full three hours away, up Highway 400 to the city of Barrie. They pulled off the highway at a Wal-Mart. MH, Mushey, and Aravena needed new shoes since they had thrown theirs into the bonfire along with all of the clothing they had worn through the night. All they could afford were flip-flops, a few bags of chips, and some bottles of water. They didn't know it, but by this time the cops were already watching the Kellestine farm; they had gotten out of there just in time.

Sandham had time for a short nap in the Jimmy while the others went shopping. Despite having no sleep over the past couple of days, he didn't trust anyone else to drive his truck. When the boys returned, they got back on the highway and continued on toward Winnipeg, another 20-some hours away.

When they were far enough away from civilization, Mushey rolled down the window and threw out a set of keys and shortly after they found a truck stop where they could park for a while, clean up, and talk. The trucker showers were cheap enough for them and Mushey had bought some Head & Shoulders back at the Wal-Mart in Barrie. He had heard that the shampoo removes gunshot residue. This was the first shower any of them had in two weeks and, while it felt good to be under the warming jets, they wouldn't ever be able to wash away the previous night.

So at the time the arrests were going down at the Kellestine residence, these guys were standing around the parking lot of the truck stop trying to come up with their "story." They agreed to say that they were at Kellestine's but left before the night of the party, taking a leisurely drive back instead of the one they were doing now in haste.

MH, Sandham, and Mushey stepped aside for a while as they chatted since they still considered Aravena as a "non-Bandido." MH and Sandham were worried that Aravena would rat and wouldn't be able to keep to the story.

As they climbed back in the Jimmy, MH asked Aravena how he was doing.

"How do you think I'm doing?" Aravena chimed back with fear in his eyes. MH responded with a guffaw and then did what is common in biker culture so that wiretaps can't pick up information. He gestured. His gesture was of a guy riding a horse, which he then followed by drawing his index finger across his throat. MH was apparently telling Aravena that he had killed one of the men from the Toronto Bandidos, a guy nicknamed "Pony." It sent a shudder through Aravena as MH laughed.

The arrests went down at the Kellestine farm. When the boys got back to Winnipeg, Sandham went out to rake the leaves in his garden, Aravena settled back into his room at Mushey's house, and Mushey reported in to his parole officer.

"Yes, I was at Kellestine's. No. We left Friday morning before any of that shit went down."

As an ex-cop, Sandham knew he had to take care of a few things. He went to a detailing shop to have his Jimmy's seats and carpets cleaned. He didn't know at the time that a Winnipeg police officer just happened to be at the same detailing shop that day. When Sandham went to a neighbour-hood Wal-Mart to buy new tires so that his treads couldn't be traced back to Kellestine's or Shedden, he didn't realize he was under surveillance. The store sold him new tires despite the fact that his other ones were in fine condition. It was probably a tipoff that he wanted to dispose of his own tires as well, instead of the customary practice of leaving old tires behind at the shop.

Sandham and his wife then drove out to a remote country road where he turfed the tires in a ditch. The ex-cop thought he was being pretty clever. Apparently he didn't know that Winnipeg police officers watched as he did this and quickly moved in once he drove off. They snatched the tires and replaced them with a set of dummy tires.

It wouldn't be long before they visited his home and asked him what he knew about the murders outside London. They repeatedly advised him to "come clean" as it would be in his best interest. But Sandham declined.

"I was just working out in the yard that day. My wife was with me."

Sandham now knew he was being watched. He took a leisurely drive in the country a week later to make sure his tires were still in the ditch and felt reassured when he saw a set out there.

As he became the object of more attention, he was convinced that Aravena was the one who couldn't be trusted and so he avoided all of the men for a full two weeks as he tried to figure out his next moves.

With Kellestine clearly out of the picture, charged with eight counts of first degree murder, the little man with a plan decided he needed to get the International Bandidos organization on side. In late April, he hopped on his Harley, as the Texans wouldn't take him seriously if he showed up in his Jimmy, and for some reason, the police let him cross the border as he trekked down to Houston. They didn't seem to have enough evidence yet against him, so they merely followed his every move.

By this time, Bandidos head office was saying that the Winnipeg chapter needed to be dealing with them directly rather than establishing themselves via the Washington State group as had been the case in the Peace Arch meeting.

When Sandham eventually arrived in Texas, he followed the directives he had been given to meet at a gas station where he had a full-body search in the restroom before he would have a chance to meet with the International Bandido officers. He was received warmly on the first day in a meeting with El Presidente, Jeff Pike. He thought he was in good with a significant shot at becoming the Canadian president.

The following day he received a call in his motel room asking if he had ever been a cop. Sandham flatly denied it, but his radar went up when he was met by several hours of silence from the Texans. Sandham didn't know the RCMP were down there on the same day and had alerted the Texans about Sandham's history.

Plan B: hightail it out of there before the Bandidos came for him. He got back on his Harley and headed back to the Canadian border as fast as he could. This time he was detained.

"Where were you?" the officials asked him.

"Kansas," Sandham repeatedly offered. "To visit friends." He had a whole story to go along with this tale as well, complete with fabricated names and addresses. And the border officials eventually let him go, presumably now because he was back under the surveillance of Canadian officials on Canadian soil.

Sandham may have been shaken by his trip, but he was a survivor if nothing else. He returned to Winnipeg and informed his brothers that he had gone to Texas and ironed everything out with head office, receiving confirmation that the Bandidos Winnipeg chapter was officially approved and he was both the president of this club and the national president.

The truth was that Bandidos International had cut off all ties with Canada. The Canadians had proven to be a motley lot of wannabes, snitches, and addicts. Very few of them owned bikes, none of them followed club regulations, and none of them were brothers in the true sense of the culture.

But MH, Mushey, and Aravena bought into Sandham's talk, so the boys in Winnipeg went ahead and got themselves some new patches made up. When Aravena was seen out with his patch, he apparently raised some suspicions and the police invited him in for a chat. Sandham was worried that Aravena didn't have the strength to resist the questioning. Mushey remained confident that Aravena would stick to the story. Ironically, if not stupidly, MH was the one who derided Aravena the most.

"That guy's gonna rat. He's too stupid to stick to the story."

•   •   •

Back in London, Brett Gardiner was trying to figure out how to survive jail life. He had never been detained for more than one night before and this was a considerable adjustment. Officials kept Mather, Kellestine, and Gardiner separated, so

Gardiner felt as though he didn't have a friend in the world. He regularly got into fights and was thrown in the "hole."

The hole is a four-by-six-foot cell with a mattress and a toilet. A detainee thrown into the hole might get out of there for 20 minutes a day, but even that couldn't be guaranteed. The hole in London's detention centre was far better than most. It didn't have the traditional rats of the four-legged variety that were the norm in places like Toronto's Don Jail. The toilet didn't overflow. Food was served on a regular basis. But for a 21-year-old man who had never done time, it would be hell.

Even though their relationship had been short-lived, Mushey had always been Gardiner's protector. He took him under his wing, he ensured that the young man understood complexities, and, most importantly, he helped Gardiner keep his cool when others were losing theirs. Gardiner no longer had an overseer and friend beside him.

On a couple of occasions he was able to reach his trusted protector who now told Gardiner that his probationary patch awaited him on his release.

Gardiner merely shook his head into the phone and smoothed back his dark hair.

"I've seen too much in 21 years, D. I don't want this shit no more. I don't want the life. I just want to go home."

As always, Mushey assured him that everything was going to be okay.

•   •   •

While Sandham thought either Aravena or Gardiner was giving information, and Mushey was sure that neither would, MH's little secret had matured into a full-fledged covert operation. By April 15, just a few days before Sandham's road trip to Texas, he fessed up to his buddy Tim Dyack that he was indeed at the Kellestine farm the night that the murders took place and could give the cop lots of detail.

How is it that Sandham was able to cross the border when MH had already told them about his involvement in the murders?

While Sandham was desperately trying to figure out how to manipulate others in a highly volatile situation, MH saw himself as *the* bringer of justice. Perhaps it occurred to him that he might be better off committing fully to his police informant's role if he wanted to save himself from a lengthy penitentiary sentence; it might have been that day that Officer Dyack told him, "Either you're on the bus or you're under it." And it might have been the sweet deal offered by Officer Dyack that if he came clean, he could get somewhere in the neighbourhood of $750,000. So MH decided it was in his best interest to get *on* the bus. That meant everyone else was going under it, whether they deserved to or not.

Dyack, having now received the assurance from MH that he would report the entirety of the evening as well as all of the events leading up to it, handed his trusted informant over to become a full agent. On April 16, fewer than 10 days after the murders, MH met with two new officers (or "handlers") and revised his original statement of absolute innocence in a four-hour audio-videotaped interview. Detective Constable Jeff Gateman and Detective Sergeant Mark Loader of the OPP Biker Enforcement Unit were now charged with the task of getting MH prepared to be a full agent. MH needed to learn how to get people to talk while he was wearing a body pack (a concealed audio recording device), he needed to know how to call for help if he was in danger, and he needed to know where and when to meet with his handlers to describe what had taken place each day.

In May, MH talked up a storm.

In his video-recorded statement with Gateman and Loader, he identified himself as only ever having been a witness and a driver, often with something of a disturbing joviality. Apparently the confession he had made to Aravena about being one of the killers was not to be entered into his statement.

May was a busy month for MH beyond just the talking. MH began now to make trips with his handlers along the route from Winnipeg to Kellestine's farm. As they drove the route from Winnipeg to London, MH showed them the reverse order of their trip home from Kellestine's. He showed them where they had taken their showers, where they had picked up the flip-flops and Head & Shoulders shampoo, where keys were thrown out of the Jimmy, where they stopped for an ice cream or some other food. When they got to the Kellestine farm, he toured them through the house and out to the barn where the murders had taken place, including showing them a crack in the cement floor where blood had been swept. He showed them the jug of muriatic acid and provided details on how the floor had been cleaned. He described where the police scanners were and told his handlers where each of the murdered men sat or stood during the night. He described, in detail, the order of the vehicles leaving Kellestine's property and the route they had taken with their "passengers" before they wound up on the side of the road outside of Shedden. He showed them where keys had been tossed out of vehicles after the bodies were dumped. He reviewed the events of the night—but with big gaps in his memory.

He especially seemed sketchy about who the killers were in those early statements.

MH knew, however, that he had to give them what they wanted to hear. He told them there was a plan to murder and that Kellestine had indicated this through a statement of "Kill one, kill 'em all." At first, MH reported merely that he thought Kellestine said this but wasn't sure if he had just said "Kill'em all." With every new statement uttered, the number of times those sentiments were allegedly spoken by Kellestine increased. Why did MH feel it was so important to show that his brothers had intended murder? Probably because it gave him a better case to enter witness protection and ensure that he wasn't under anyone's bus. There would be a lot of people trying to run him over.

The cops wanted Kellestine, Sandham, and Mushey because these guys were the most dangerous. It was a fair exchange to let MH go. Set one free. Bring down three. If the three others who were just there that night went down, that would be a statistical bonus. So, it seems, goes the game with an informant.

On June 9, MH became a protected witness and began working much more in concert with his handlers. It turns out that these officers spelled out different conditions for MH than Dyack had suggested. MH would *not* be receiving the three-quarters of a million dollars, and if he admitted to having pulled a trigger that night, he would lose his immunity and be convicted. If his statements ever deviated he could be charged with perjury.

He signed his immunity agreement with the Attorney General of Ontario. The agreement indicated that if MH varied at all during either the preliminary trial or the trial itself from his sworn statements of April 16, he would be opening himself up to conviction.

Paragraph 17 of the agreement spelled this out clearly:

> [MH] shall provide, if requested by the Crown, sworn truthful testimony, voluntarily at the preliminary inquiry or inquiries and trial or trials of Messrs. Marcelo Aravena, Brett Gardiner, Wayne Kellestine, Frank Mather, Dwight Mushey and Michael

Sandham, or any other person implicated on the facts and to answer any questions ruled proper by the judge in such proceedings, in a frank, complete and truthful manner.

It was underscored by paragraph 29:

If, at the trial or trials of Messrs. Marcelo Aravena, Brett Gardiner, Wayne Kellestine, Frank Mather, Dwight Mushey and Michael Sandham, or any other person or persons who may face charges arising out of the said investigation, a) the testimony of [MH] vary substantially from any of his statements obtained pursuant to paragraph 12 of this agreement, or at the preliminary inquiry or inquiries, the Crown may take whatever steps are reasonable in the circumstances, including prosecution of [MH] for charges of perjury, contempt, attempting to obstruct justice or the giving of contradictory evidence, but at that stage, will not prosecute [MH] for the first-degree or second-degree murder.

MH's lawyer spelled out the contract in layman's terms: *the story must remain the same from the first time it is told to the last time it is told.*

But MH wasn't exactly truthful with his wife about the new conditions; instead, he told her they would be receiving $75,000 a year for going into the witness-protection program, a new car, a new residence, medical insurance, and many other perks. It was a rosy picture of a new suburban lifestyle, pretty far from the reality of a rat who would never know when the protection wells would dry up or one of his many enemies might discover him. Despite the less appealing conditions now, there was no turning back without being "under the bus" and going to prison for life.

Shortly after becoming a formal agent, on June 12 MH began wearing his body pack. He was taught the art of eliciting information from his brothers and how to report it back to his handlers. It represented both science and theatre. If he were ever facing danger, his signal to his handlers would be the kicking off of a shoe. It turns out that he did not have to remove any footwear, as his brothers sincerely trusted him. In fact, when he was hospitalized with a gallbladder attack, it was only best friends Aravena and Mushey who would visit him to wish him a speedy recovery. No family. No Dyack.

MH met with his handlers daily if not several times a day to have his body pack placed and removed and for him to recount the events of the day, including the many gestures that replaced any words in the recorded conversations. There were many of these symbols ranging from a rotating finger in the air to indicate police presence or wire tapping, to the holding up of eight fingers in reference to the Shedden massacre. The index, middle, and fourth fingers held up to form the letter *W* was a reference to Kellestine. There were many other gestures that were borrowed from sign language: tears, smiles, and expressions of thanks.

According to the protocol, MH was not to remove the recording devices once they had been planted on his body. Nor did he listen to any of the conversations until well after their recording and digital storage.

Surely MH felt quite privileged to have a position of such significance, even if it meant he was ratting out his best and only friends. It wasn't until well into the trial that he would recognize the impact of his decision on his life, the life of his family, and the grave in which he was burying his dearest friend, Mushey. After all, the witness-protection program is not a lifetime deal as most would imagine it to be. Money isn't a guarantee when trials end if the informants are found doing anything criminal, and MH was a well-known entity in a dangerous world where rats are never forgiven. For now, however, it proved a better gig than sitting in the dock with his brothers. June accordingly progressed rapidly for the police as the case came together through MH's statements.

On June 13, MH, Mushey, Sandham, and Aravena were all out for a stroll in Winnipeg proudly wearing their leather vests and Bandidos patches, albeit homemade because Texas still refused to recognize the chapter. Aravena was a prospect now, even though he was far from pleased with the way in which he had arrived here; phone calls with friends would indicate that he felt he had no choice now but to be part of the organization. He would not divulge what he had witnessed in those conversations, but he made it clear that there was no turning back time or turning his back on his brothers.

Mushey, MH, and Sandham all had their full-patches. As per the international standard, the top patch read "Bandidos," the centre patch was the Fat Mexican, and the bottom rocker now read "Canada" instead of "Probationary." To the left of the Fat Mexican was a small diamond-shaped patch with "1%" and to the right was a similar patch with "MC."

With Kellestine under arrest and detained in London, Sandham pretended he was now the Canadian president even if the Bandidos headquarters wanted him dead and wanted nothing to do with the Canadians. Mushey assumed the vice-presidency. MH, despite being an agent, now considered himself the national sergeant-at-arms. Later, Sandham would try to convince the jury he, all the while, was merely trying to establish himself so that he could become a secret agent. It seems that both MH and Sandham remained confused about whether they were "good guys" or "bad guys." Certainly neither understood the concept of brotherhood. This was a time marked by mixed emotions—fear, pride, humility, achievement … and more fear.

In the hours of audio recordings that MH brought back to the police, Sandham was both self-described as "the political mind of the chapter" and discussed by MH and Mushey as untrustworthy. Aravena was similarly and ironically derided by

MH as "the weakest link," a man with little intellect and less allegiance. MH described them as potential rats while Mushey agreed, and the conversation was recorded and then transcribed.

When Mushey felt he had allegiance, he would gladly take up an oath of loyalty to that individual or ideal. He had especially always taken care of MH and he had no reason to think that his brother would have cause to betray him.

Instead of returning respect and loyalty, the newly appointed agent painted his friend to his handlers as malevolent, calculating, and lacking in any conscience. It was a portrait that media reporters quickly accepted as truth, sealed Mushey's fate, and underscored the greatest act of betrayal throughout the entire trial. MH would have to shore this treachery in his conscience for the balance of his life.

The arrests started the evening of Thursday, June 15, at Dwight Mushey's home, and ended the morning of Friday, June 16, at Michael Sandham's.

Because Sandham had his phone turned off through the night, a cellphone was fired through his front window on the morning of June 16, shattering glass on one of his children who was sleeping below.

Questioning followed while both he and his wife were sequestered.

Mushey said nothing. Aravena said nothing. Sandham did a lot of disclaiming, at one point even threatening that he would sue the police. It seems he didn't concern himself with the fact that his wife was potentially being charged as an accomplice and that his children would wind up without parents around to rear them.

Despite the officer's repeated suggestions that Sandham "be a man" (tell the truth) and make sure his wife would not be charged, Sandham continued to refuse any knowledge or participation. If he really did want to become a police informant, a "double agent," this was his last chance and he was blowing it.

CHAPTER 10
The Theatre

When we are born, we cry that we
are come
To this great stage of fools.

—*King Lear*, act 4, scene 6

Nobody will ever know exactly what happened the night of April 7, 2006. Not the men there that night. Not the police who tried to piece together the murder of eight men after the fact.

Dead men don't speak. Real bikers don't rat. Cops need a clean story.

The Crown would depend upon MH to tell the story. The media would only tell his (and the Crown's) side. And the jury would be heavily influenced by the Crown's portrayal of two Canadian chapters of Bandidos duking it out. It was far easier to say that the Winnipeg "gang" (eventually called "the farm team" by prosecution) was up against the Toronto "gang" (known as "The No Surrender Crew") than to try to explain the many relationships at play or to try to engage in the intricacies of an international organization at war with its own factions, the many virtually innocent individuals caught up in a political ploy, the insidiousness of drug abuse, and the nuances of egos.

The prosecution team built its case as a war between two groups, a planned execution of the No Surrender Crew. That was a good story built largely on the fiction of MH. While it is easy to argue that organized crime is organized, that is far from the truth of what went down on April 7.

While some of the locals at the Holland House chatted about the hockey game, while the Steeles readied to bed themselves down for the night in their comfortable home outside of Shedden, and while the Toronto Bandidos began their two-hour drive out to the location just west of London, the Kellestine farmhouse was preparing for its visitors.

Church would take place in the central room of Wayne's barn, where churches were historically held; since Gardiner, Aravena, and Mather were not even prospective Bandidos, they were to simply remain in the farmhouse.

This was not a farmer's barn by any stretch of the imagination. It was cluttered with old couches, chairs, tables, and mattresses. There was a chest freezer with a dead rabbit inside and there were efforts to set up some sort of two-way radio between the house and the barn. The two-way radio never materialized and only communication from the house could be directed to the barn. After all, the most important communication would come from the house where Gardiner was supposedly tending to one of the police scanners and would need to advise anyone if there was police surveillance on the farm that night. He likely didn't know why and he never asked. In the two weeks preceding this night, he only knew that Kellestine was paranoid, closing the gate to his enclosure (though it apparently didn't lock) and conducting his own surveillance walking the perimeter of the property with a shotgun every night or sending Aravena and Gardiner out to conduct the armed patrol.

Kellestine did not know that Aravena and Gardiner typically didn't take this job very seriously and, once out of eyesight, just lay down in the grass and looked up at the stars, planning their futures and laughing about the films they had watched that day on television. The police scanner was always on, 24-7, and Kellestine even had a portable one that he took with him any time he left the house. They just accepted Kellestine's paranoia as part of his quirky personality and questionable past.

There was a significant glitch in the plan to have Gardiner tend the scanner that night and report any police activity to the barn; Brett wouldn't know how to decipher the police communications that came over it since they were typically highly cryptic codes. It's perhaps why, despite there being considerable police attention focused on Kellestine's farm that night, Gardiner would only ever report to the barn that a police cruiser was conducting radar on the nearby highway.

As they prepared for their guests, Sandham donned a baby-blue bulletproof vest with a trauma plate duct-taped onto it that he had brought from Winnipeg, and ascended a ladder in the barn leading to a loft where he could conceal himself amid all of the old, miscellaneous furniture and household items that were flung there. MH and Mushey were perturbed that Sandham had brought a vest; if he was in fact their leader, why hadn't he warned them to prepare similarly? Because there was no safe place to hide inside the barn, MH and Mushey stood out in the field behind it, suffering the gusts of the cold evening, each carrying a shotgun but not even knowing if they worked.

Despite talking of "expecting the worst" given the No Surrender Crew's refusal to the Houston headquarters to relegate their patches and chapter, nobody really knew what lay ahead that night, certainly not the three in the house who were merely told there was some business that needed to be conducted and that these men were not in a position to have any knowledge about the nature of that business.

They only knew that the "big guys" were in town and that they would eventually be called out to impress them if they were to become Bandidos members, if that was even their intention.

MH and Mushey merely thought that only a couple of the men would be asked to give up their patches and return any Bandido property since Kellestine had regularly said there were several members he wanted to retain in the club.

If there was a drug transfer going down, it seems only Sandham and Kellestine were aware of it. Maybe only Kellestine.

If there were in fact murders ordered by the Bandidos headquarters, again, only Sandham and Kellestine had this knowledge.

As the Toronto vehicles began to roll in after nightfall, each with two members per and all arriving between 9 and 11 p.m., Kellestine greeted them warmly just outside the house, offering them beer, chatting about the tensions with the U.S. office, and suggesting that he would help with a plan of action to save the Bandidos Canada.

Sandham had taken cover among the old mattresses and furniture in the loft of the barn, his .303 rifle ready for action.

Wayne welcomed each of the men as they arrived, two by two, before he walked them out to the barn where the church was to take place. So just who were these guys who showed up that night?

Eight people in total from Toronto and its environs eventually assembled: John "Boxer" Muscedere, Luis "Chopper"

Raposo, George "Crash" Kriarakis, Frank "Bammer" Salerno, Paul "Big Pauly" Sinopoli, Jamie "Goldberg" Flanz, George "Pony" Jessome, and Michael "Little Mikey" Trotta.

Muscedere was the true old-time biker of the lot. He was a good old boy who loved the camaraderie. Kellestine had long been his mentor and Muscedere learned from the best that your brothers are more important than anything else. At home, his beautiful wife Nina waited for his return. He also had two daughters who could easily rival Italian runway models, and he had grandchildren who were the centre of his life. His children and grandchildren had experienced a number of tragedies, but he was always the man to whom they could turn.

Raposo, his handsome Mediterranean sidekick, was also there, hopped up on cocaine and ready for action. He had never wanted a Winnipeg chapter established and once he found out Sandham had been a cop, he had some serious reckoning he deemed necessary. He was eager to arrive.

Salerno, a guy from Oakville with a loving wife and brand-new baby son, had shot enough heroin into his arm to give him a peaceful, easy feeling as they pulled in that night. Despite rumours that he had wanted to leave the club, he was clearly confused about his future. When the Texan Bandidos had disenfranchised Toronto back in December, he had written an emotional e-mail in response. "I'm sitting here feeling confused, dejected, emotionally drained" was his response to the Texan directive. Salerno's wife was the one to pen many of his thoughtful e-mails. Though it is the norm that one's wife is not involved in Bandidos affairs, she was his confidante and protector. He was a loving husband and father, and she knew he had a future once he kicked his habit.

If in fact a hit was ordered on him by the head office, perhaps it was because of the heroin or because of his defiance.

"Little Mikey" Trotta was a good friend of Salerno. His common-law wife was a grade-school teacher and he was the manager of a used-trailer sales and rental facility. Nicknamed for his small stature, he was merely a hangaround with the Bandidos and had likely only come this night as an act of friendship. He should never have been attending a church, but then, Toronto was notorious for breaking rules. At 31 years old, he seemed to have his middle-class suburban life ahead of him. None of his neighbours and colleagues would have ever considered Trotta a "biker," and it's debatable that even he thought of himself as such.

There was George "Pony" Jessome, an older fellow who, again, didn't have full status in the organization but was well respected by all as someone on whom they could rely. He drove a tow truck and had terminal cancer. He'd only been hanging with the Bandidos for about a year.

Then there was "Big Pauly" Sinopoli, aptly named because he weighed in between 400 and 500 pounds, had several chins, and invariably struggled with numerous health issues because of his weight, including digestive tract problems, ulcers, and diabetes.

George "Crash" Kriarakis had been a stable member of the organization for years. Coincidentally, when Muscedere was travelling in Italy some time ago, the Texas Bandidos appointed Kriarakis Canadian president because they knew they could count on him. He was a handsome man of Greek descent with a loving, well-established Greek Orthodox family. His father was a traditionalist. His mother, an articulate and well-educated woman who stood fast in her ideals of righteousness. But when Muscedere returned from Italy, Muscedere swiftly resumed his status as president of Canada, refusing to relinquish it despite what headquarters had demanded. That would have been another reason for Texas to want to be rid of Muscedere. Kriarakis acquiesced and accepted the Toronto presidential position in lieu of the national presidency.

The last of the Toronto boys to come that night, Jamie Flanz, had travelled from Sutton, about an hour north of Toronto, where he was attempting to restore his life. His wife Michelle and their two young children had moved to the United States where he could not visit them because of an outstanding U.S. criminal charge and, more recently, the murder investigation of a small-time drug dealer at Flanz's home.

He was the director of an information technology staffing company while trying to form his own firm, and driving a tow truck on the side to try to make ends meet. It is difficult to imagine how a relatively young man who hailed from Montreal's upperclass could have wound up where he was tonight.

The shore of Lake Simcoe, where Sutton is situated, was lined with prosperous estate homes, but farther inland the town grew seedy. Flanz had moved there nine years ago from Quebec where his father was senior partner in a law firm and where Flanz had grown up as an avid hockey player. His family had no idea that he was involved in a bike gang, but they did know that he had been in trouble and was trying to turn his life around, including reconciliation with his wife.

It was Flanz who had, according to the one theory about stolen drugs, found the Hells Angels' cocaine. It was Flanz who the police were following that night out to Kellestine's because a drug dealer had been murdered in his home recently. The dealer had sold a sister of one of the Bandidos some dope, an apparent offence, and the fellow paid handsomely for his sin.

It was Flanz that Wayne Kellestine had the least use for.

Because Flanz was a Jew. And Wayne was convinced Flanz was a rat.

• • •

There the group of men: Sandham in the loft with his loaded weapon, MH and Mushey in the field behind the barn, Aravena, Mather, and Gardiner cuddled up inside the house watching movies. The other eight standing or sitting in the barn.

Even though Gardiner was presumably ordered to listen to the police scanner, it was neither something to take seriously given Kellestine's paranoia nor was it a task to be performed by someone who wasn't trained appropriately in monitoring police conversations.

Before the church started, Flanz was admiring the firearm Raposo had brought with him. Raposo turned to him and laughed. "It's to put a big fucking hole in that fucking pig," he said, meaning his intention to kill Sandham. Sandham heard it.

Sandham was either the sniper or the sitting duck.

As the new visitors each ventured out to the barn, they found seats in the various old sofas and chairs.

As MH and Mushey stood shivering behind the barn, peering through a hole in the barnboard, the evening's events unfolded. Wayne was in his element orchestrating the church from the middle of the barn and all started amicably enough.

Once the Toronto eight had seated themselves in the barn, Kellestine began the church with his key message. He informed them that he was the new national president by orders of the international headquarters in Houston. The Toronto members were then ordered to give up their patches and all Bandidos property.

Angry and resentful, the Toronto eight confronted Kellestine. Sandham stood up in the loft and loaded ammunition into the chamber of his .303 rifle with a loud click. Muscedere and Raposo heard it above the commotion. Muscedere, always the caretaker for Raposo, shielded him as Raposo drew his sawed-off shotgun and aimed it into the loft. A flurry of firing ensued. Sandham was the second to fire, shooting a single bullet at Raposo that travelled a strange but lethal trajectory. The bullet struck Raposo's finger, sending fragments of bone and shrapnel into his chest and neck. Ironically it was the middle finger he had always held up in photos indicating his air of defiance. He would never be able to gesture a "fuck you" again.

Another shot or two was rapidly fired, who knows by whom since Kellestine may not have had a weapon at this point. Salerno received a wound to the leg, Kriarakis to the abdomen. Trotta's scalp was grazed by shot, likely mistakenly delivered by Raposo. Even though Kellestine pummelled and kicked Trotta several times through the night, it was the wounds to his scalp that caused his eyes to swell profusely and bruise, something the forensic specialists would refer to as "raccoon eyes." His left eye virtually swelled shut as the night progressed, the blood from his scalp slowly seeping down into his sinus cavities.

Once the shooting broke out, Mushey and MH hustled into the barn. Or were they already inside despite MH's testimony? Had it been MH's gun that went off, wounding Salerno and Kriarakis?

Mather had heard the shots in the house and grabbed a shotgun from the worn pool table where the weapons had been assembled as he ran toward the barn. Aravena followed fast on Mather's heels armed only with a baseball bat. During the investigation, there was considerable speculation that MH had already been in the barn when the shots were fired and that he may have been the one to fire a shot or two.

As Raposo gasped for breath and bled profusely from the neck and chest, making gurgling sounds as he tried to speak, Kellestine ordered all of the Toronto members to lie face down on the cement floor.

Kellestine repeatedly yelled, "Who shot first?! Who fucking shot first? I know you have three guns. Where are the fucking guns?"

Was he speculating about the number of guns or had he just been keeping more secrets? It seems more than likely he knew that the men were intending to kill Sandham and had packed accordingly.

Kellestine especially took out his anger on Flanz.

"Fucking Jew. Fucking rat," Kellestine repeated as he kicked him numerous times while he lay on the floor.

Sandham slowly descended from the loft, shaking shot pellets from his hooded sweatshirt. Apparently the bulletproof vest was a wise decision.

Kellestine cuffed him in the head and took the .303 from Sandham. "You fucking asshole!"

Sandham repeated that Raposo had shot first and the rest of the men agreed.

Kellestine repeatedly ordered Muscedere down on the floor, but Muscedere was clearly defiant.

His best friend was down and dying. And his former best friend and mentor couldn't care less.

And as Kellestine repeatedly threatened to kill "the fucking Jew," pointing his gun at Flanz's head, Muscedere tried to assure Kellestine that Flanz was a good guy.

As Raposo gurgled through blood, Kellestine steadied his gun on the men on the floor. Mather took a position in the corner of the barn, holding a shotgun he didn't even know could fire. MH and Mushey now steadied their arms on the No Surrender Crew as Kellestine ordered.

When Aravena arrived bearing just a baseball bat and his bravado, he didn't yet know there was a man dying in the corner.

Mushey and Kellestein stepped outside where Muscedere revealed that Flanz had murdered an enemy of the Bandidos in his home, a drug dealer from Keswick by the name of Shawn Douse.

"Jamie's not a rat, bro," Muscedere tried to convince Kellestine. But Kellestine wasn't convinced by the time they came back into the barn. He gave Flanz a few more kicks to the head.

"Fucking Jew. Fucking rat."

It's unclear when, but at some point Kellestine butt-stroked Muscedere with the end of his shotgun. Muscedere was missing his two front teeth now.

At this point, Gardiner remained in the farmhouse. He knew he would not be welcomed in the barn and simply stood his post by the police scanner as he had been ordered.

Sandham moved into the main room where all were assembled, and he apologized to Salerno for shooting Raposo. Salerno acknowledged the need for defensive action and accepted the apology, even though it was likely not heartfelt in that Sandham had just seriously wounded the man who, just minutes ago, had boasted he was going to "put a big fucking hole in the fucking pig."

Muscedere begged to take Raposo to the hospital. Kellestine refused. Muscedere paced as Kellestine ordered MH to search the men and take all of their belongings out of their pockets. Face down on the floor, the men had no choice but to give up their cellphones, their wallets, their keys, and any Bandidos property. MH seemed to enjoy his chance to belittle his brothers, kicking Sinopoli in the head as he searched him. Mushey was ordered to shoot any of the men if they moved. Clearly he didn't follow this directive as Muscedere alternately rose, sat, fretted, paced, and swore. Raposo continued to gurgle and then ceased to make any sounds. Trotta was ordered to make a list of the possessions, especially any Bandidos property.

Raposo was the first to die. Aravena moved cautiously closer as his curiosity melded with anxiety.

"I never seen a dead man before."

Once it was clear that Raposo was dead, all of the men kneeled and said the Lord's Prayer by his body. Plans were made to have Salerno dispose of the body since Salerno knew of some old wells that the men had previously used for such a purpose. The rest of the men would be driven home that night where any other Bandidos property would be seized.

Muscedere, meanwhile, was convinced that Raposo wasn't going to be the only one to die. He rose to challenge Kellestine. "Take me first. Do me like a man," he repeated as he also told his colleagues to "quit whining."

In true biker style, Muscedere demanded machismo from his brothers.

"We didn't sign up for some fucking Boy Scout club. We knew what we faced when we joined."

As he repeatedly requested that Kellestine just "shoot me like a man," he dismissed Kriarakis's praying and crying despite the fact that his brother was suffering a very painful wound to the abdomen. Perhaps he didn't realize that many of his brothers had not signed up for this aspect of "the life." They had signed up for camaraderie. Not exactly the Lion's Club, but also not the Hells Angels.

Muscedere was a lead actor. His brothers were merely players on the stage that had been set for them.

Now the king had a conundrum. Raposo was dead. Muscedere, the natural successor, was asking to be killed. Three of the others had been wounded. If he were hopped up on crystal meth, Kellestine couldn't possibly sort out those he had previously deemed "salvageable" and those who might turn against him. To resolve his quandary, he called Sandham and Mushey outside the barn for a series of discussions.

There were no recordings of the actual conversations, however many there were (whether three or four) that took place outside of the barn that night where decisions were made. But details drawn together piecemeal from court testimony provide ample evidence that Kellestine suggested at some point during the meetings that execution of Muscedere was necessary; Sandham lacked the backbone to speak, and only Mushey stood in defiance that this was not the Bandidos way.

But clearly the Bandidos way had long been lost.

CHAPTER 11

Nightfall

Things that love night, love not nights
like these.

— *King Lear*, act 3, scene 2

When animals respond to predators, it ultimately comes down to fight or flight. But sometimes, the prey freezes in its tracks.

Locked up inside Wayne Kellestine's fences and the many fields that stood so far from civilization, flight was not an option for any of the men herein contained this night, not the men from Winnipeg and not the men from Toronto and its environs.

At the Kellestine farm that evening was a cast of individuals with different aspirations, needs, demons, and desires, and seemingly only Sandham and Kellestine held the men's fate in their hands. Though Mushey was asked out of the barn to a couple of the meetings where decisions were seemingly being made, he was also clearly unsure about who might die that night. When he returned to the inner sanctum of the barn, he merely said to MH, "Be ready."

Only in retrospect would MH understand that, as always, Mushey was watching out for him.

Once Raposo had, beyond any doubt, died, Kellestine ordered Trotta and Flanz to roll up his body in an old carpet and haul it out to one of the cars. Raposo's dead weight was difficult for the men, but they did as they were told according to biker code. No requests, only orders. Muscedere stepped in to help his brothers carry the load as they dropped the body several times. Flanz's fingers were nearly numb from the cold and he could not keep his grasp on the carpet. They eventually loaded up the lifeless body into the trunk of a Volkswagen.

The balance of the night did not have a clear directive, but rather consisted of a series of actions taken largely by men who did not know when or if they were next to die. If they followed this biker code, it may have merely been to save their own lives; if anything was certain that night, it was uncertainty.

To add to the uncertainty, Kellestine even broke into song, the Nazi national anthem, which was the first stanza of the German anthem "Das Lied der Deutshen," also called "Deutschland uber alles." He danced the same jig that he danced at many Bandidos parties and recorded on numerous video tapes.

Apparently he wasn't feeling much remorse for Raposo's death.

Once the body had been removed, whatever prompted Gardiner to leave his post in the house monitoring the police scanner, whether it was fear or curiosity, he went to the barn unarmed and stood beside his friend, Mushey.

Mushey knew what would happen. Araveno, Gardiner, and Mather were completely oblivious to the plans for Muscedere, if indeed there were any.

Kellestine passed his shotgun over to Sandham. Since Muscedere was the most insolent of the lot, Kellestine brought out an old set of shackles that linked handcuffs to ankle irons. He passed them to Aravena to hold as he led Muscedere out of the barn and instructed Marcelo to follow.

"Not that I don't trust you," Kellestine said to Muscedere, "but I don't trust you."

Apparently the mistrust was mutual. Kellestine took the lead out of the barn calling Aravena, who was now armed only with a flashlight and his cocky fighting instincts, to take up the rear.

"I knew I could take him if he tried anything," Aravena eventually reported. "He was a has-been fighter."

The three exited the barn and shuffled down the laneway to the Toronto vehicles.

Muscedere was led to the front of the Volkswagen where the door was opened and he was ordered by the new national president to sit in the passenger's seat.

Muscedere declined. "I get in there and you're gonna put two holes in the back of my head."

"Look, bro," Kellestine assured him. "We just need to make you look like a passenger. We'll drive you home and get your patches and stuff. Okay?"

Muscedere then stepped into the vehicle as Aravena watched on with his flashlight fixed.

Aravena's eyes grew wide in disbelief as Kellestine pulled a handgun out of a pocket inside of his coat.

There were indeed two shots to the head as Muscedere had anticipated. The first did not kill him and, according to Aravena's testimony, "he grinned back at Wayne like he knew he was the real man and Wayne was not a real biker." The second bullet proved successful, a bullet travelling from one ear to the other; Kellestine then followed with a shot to the abdomen where the bullet grazed Muscedere's liver and perforated his heart and left lung. His mouth gaped open showing the injuries to his lower lip and inside of the mouth where the two teeth had been broken.

He went out like a man. Smiling at the devil before he died.

Aravena was speechless, nauseous, and nearly toppled over at the sight and smell.

Kellestine waved the handgun at Araveno.

"Put that fucking piece of shit's leg in the car."

Muscedere, the former best friend, the one Kellestine had sponsored decades ago to become a 1%er. Aravena had never seen a dead man before, let alone someone executed. The next moments were blurred by his shock, but he did as he was instructed under the watchful eyes of the crazed commander. Aravena clearly had no choice.

As Kellestine headed back to the barn, Aravena hurried into the house. He wanted to tell Gardiner what he had just witnessed, but Gardiner was not at his post.

Meanwhile in the barn, oblivious to any plans that had been made, Gardiner heard the shots as his head spun in the direction of the cars outside. "Did you hear that?!" his head rapidly swinging back to Mushey. "I should go check on W!"

"Shut up and get back in the fucking house," Mushey snapped at Gardiner in anger.

Because of Gardiner's unknowing blunder, the Toronto members had now been alerted and Mushey was instantly concerned about the safety of the men to whom he was loyal. Gardiner followed Mushey's order and quickly left the barn, heading back inside the house.

When Kellestine returned to the barn, he moved to the radio and turned up the volume; Sandham took him outside and told him about Gardiner's slip-up. It's likely that Sandham and Kellestine thought the young man who they had previously sent out in search of a pickle tree was not smart enough to be trusted and should also be shot. Gardiner was, as per his custom, kept in the dark about what had just happened.

Somehow Gardiner and Aravena must have missed each other between the house and the barn. After witnessing

Muscedere's execution and Kellestine's clear violence, Aravena didn't feel safe in the house by himself and wanted to be as close as possible to the men whom he thought he could trust, Sandham, Mushey, and MH. He knew he couldn't trust Kellestine.

Arriving at the barn, he encountered Sandham just outside where he breathlessly reported the witnessing of Muscedere's death. "I just saw W smoke Boxer! He just whacked Boxer!" he exclaimed.

"Get yourself together, bro," Sandham attempted to reassure him. "Boxer's the only one."

Perhaps no other decisions had been made yet. Or perhaps Sandham was, according to his custom, not being entirely truthful.

Back inside the barn, Kellestine was doing more dancing and singing, Kriarakis was praying in Greek as he rocked on a chair he had been permitted to move to because of his abdominal wound, Flanz was ordered to sit cross-legged with his hands above his head, Sinopoli was peeing frequently in the corner of the barn; his diabetes and the gunshot wound to the leg were taking their tolls on his bladder. Trotta's eye was swelling shut. Aravena took pity on Kriarakis and tossed him a blanket; MH responded to Araveno's benevolence with a disapproving glare. Maybe that wasn't a manly thing to do?

Eventually Kellestine ordered Trotta and Flanz to get up off the floor and clean up Raposo's blood. With an old blanket and a makeshift mop, they tried to push the blood into a crack in the cement. They weren't particularly successful, merely making more of a mess.

Perhaps there was one more meeting outside with Kellestine, Sandham, and Mushey. We can't be sure.

Inside the barn, however, it was decided by all of the men, Kellestine included, that Jessome would take Kriarakis and Sinopoli to a hospital in Toronto's west end where gunshot wounds would be more common than in London. Jessome could drive them there and just leave them by the Emergency entrance. And because Jessome was old and had terminal cancer, it wouldn't matter much if he were arrested in carrying out this task.

But promises in this culture can be short lived.

Kellestine led the way for a grateful Kriarakis, while, according to Aravena's eventual testimony, MH followed closely behind, carrying his shotgun. Kriarakis stepped into the front of the Volkswagen and seated himself there with considerable pain in the driver's seat. He would have smelled the blood from the two other bodies in the car just before his own execution.

Wayne produced the concealed handgun and now fired six shots: two to Kriarakis's temple, one to his face where the bullet lodged in his forehead, and three more to the torso. What could Wayne have been thinking killing this guy while he occupied the driver's seat? How would they now dispose of the body? Again, if this were something planned, it certainly wasn't *well* planned.

And, of course, MH could never confess to seeing this execution.

At first MH's statements claimed he didn't know who went out with Kellestine and Kriarakis. Even during the preliminary trial, he said he wasn't sure. After several years and many testimonies later, he fingered best friend Mushey in a highly unlikely shift in the story. Eventually he would even testify that Mushey was the actual killer. Scouring through his many statements, one has to wonder why he eventually felt it necessary to implicate someone else. Instead, his statements shifted to him being the one to care for Kriarakis that night with a blanket, and he would never admit to kicking him in the head when they were ordered to the ground.

Aravena's version seemed far more likely: that Aravena took care of the weakening Kriarakis, prior to MH and Kellestine leading him to his death.

With Kriarakis guided out to die as he occupied the driver's seat of the Volkswagen, the group would need to consider how they might eventually get the vehicle off the property. MH, Sandham, and Kellestine tried to hook up the car to the tow truck. Mushey refused to participate. By now Raposo, Muscedere, and Kriarakis were all lifeless within the small vehicle.

The three living men assembled by the tow truck, but were unable to operate the winch. They returned to the barn where they asked Jessome to come and help hook up the car to the tow truck. Jessome was informed that Kriarakis was waiting for him in the Volkswagen.

MH, Sandham, and Kellestine told Jessome that Kriarakis needed to be less visible and so was asked to sit in what would be the towed Volkswagon. Jessome, of course, didn't know that Kriarakis was now the dead driver of that vehicle.

An aging gentleman who had come to accept that he was going to die of his cancer in the near future, Jessome wanted to help get his brothers the aid they needed. So he joined the men where he hooked up the winch to the Volkswagen and climbed into the truck's back seat on the driver's side. He was told that he would just need to wait there for Sinopoli. It was Pony's last act of kindness.

This time, if MH's confession to Aravena on the way back to Winnipeg was accurate, Kellestine handed MH the handgun. MH's tearful recounting of his version on the stand fingered Mushey as the one to have shot Kriarakis, while MH himself was only a shocked witness to Jessome's murder. But too many pieces of his puzzle didn't connect and too many tears were shed over Jessome.

As deranged as Kellestine may have been that night, he surely would not have been the one to do all of the killing. That would arguably leave him far too vulnerable, not likely of someone so typically cunning; he would not require hangarounds Aravena and Gardiner to do anything or require much of the mere roommate, Mather . . . but Sandham, MH, and Mushey were members, and full participation under the leadership would be required.

Jessome took five shots. One was to the left cheek at close range from left to right and slightly upward. Another shot was fired to his left temple, slightly upward and from back to front. Another was close range to the left temple, upward and front to back. He then had been shot in the left chest at close range from left to right, front to back, and sharply upward.

Forensics also indicated that Jessome had an abrasion to his right wrist, hand, and middle finger caused by a .22-calibre bullet. That final evidence would suggest that MH was in the barn when the shooting first broke out, and that his Mossberg .22 was one of the guns that rang out with the shots after Raposo and Sandham. It would explain why there were more than two shots that rang out at the beginning of that night.

MH then could not have actually been outside the barn in the field when Raposo was shot.

Would the defence team of lawyers be able to make this clear to the jury? They would be successful in having him termed an "unsavoury witness" by the judge, which, in legal terms, means the jury was eventually instructed not to trust his account. But it seemed the defence team would not focus on MH's involvement so early on in the evening.

The jury members would not know about the many incongruities in MH's statements from his first accounts through preliminary trial to the final trial. Instead, the jury members were overwhelmed with information throughout the trial. They would miss the nuances. They would not be given the opportunity to think through MH's participation.

The jury would not, in such a short period of deliberation time and with so much information to process, understand that

MH contributed to the many injuries early on and conclude that MH was Jessome's killer.

MH should have been with his brothers in that courtroom instead of facing them from the stand. He should have been facing eight counts of first-degree murder instead of spinning tales. He should have been going to jail instead of getting a new identity and a paycheque every month.

Love ya, bro.

Get under the bus.

•   •   •

Perhaps because Salerno was loaded up on heroin, he met his end with stoicism and relative calmness. He took a phone call from his wife and told her he would be home soon. He asked how the new baby was and told her he loved them both. Then he extended his hand to Mushey who politely shook it and nodded a respectful farewell.

"Nice to know you, man," they said.

MH cowardly looked away and refused the extended hand.

Sandham reported that he would not shake Salerno's hand because it was covered in blood, while Aravena similarly did not want to get blood on his clothing. Aravena, after all, still thought everyone but Muscedere and Raposo were going home that night and Mushey was showing an air of defiance to the plan Sandham and Kellestine had laid.

Sandham was merely acting in the same self-interest he had always evinced; he didn't want to get any "evidence" on his body.

Salerno uttered his final words. "Tell my family where the body is."

Kellestine called to Mushey to follow. Mushey refused to participate. Kellestine knew best not to take on Mushey, so he turned instead to call upon Sandham.

After Mushey shook Salerno's hand, he merely stepped back. MH said Mushey followed Salerno out, a blatant lie. Instead, Sandham was the accompanist according to his own testimony.

After a brief walk down the laneway to the silver Infiniti vehicle, Salerno gently seated himself in the back seat and looked at Kellestine; according to Sandham's testimony, the look was tender. He was shot between the eyes at close range, the bullet ricocheting inside his skull and breaking apart, though no one can be certain who pulled the trigger this time. Because he was shot with two different guns, one being the sidearm with which Sandham was most familiar, it is highly likely that Sandham fired at least one of the bullets.

Perhaps Salerno's last thoughts were of his new baby, his home in Oakville, and the error he had made in remaining in the club long after he had envisioned his departure.

Sinopoli, the next to be led out, was followed by the still-naive Aravena. The severely overweight man with a wounded leg was asked to haul his large frame into the cargo of the silver Infiniti. A first shot was fired, but the rear hatch dropped onto Sinopoli's arm and the rifle jammed. Aravena eventually testified that Kellestine had yelled at Sinopoli for struggling, telling him to "die like a fucking man." As Sinopoli fought to release his arm, Kellestine used the point of the rifle to reopen the hatch before drawing out his handgun and again firing.

Then Kellestine turned his attention to Aravena and ordered the young hangaround to get into the car, to which Aravena shrewdly and boldly declined. Kellestine responded by holding the rifle to Araveno's chest. His words and appearance were menacing.

"I ain't doing 25 years for you, Fat Ass," sneered Kellestine. "If you tell anyone, I'll kill you and your family."

The reminder Kellestine gave to Aravena the next day on his departure was intended to affirm the threat.

Aravena had no reason to doubt the warning after what he had just witnessed. He responded appropriately, "I ain't saying shit. I ain't a rat." He repeated it several times until Kellestine moved the gun away from his chest.

Then Aravena turned and walked quickly away to the house, his heart and mind racing. He paced alone and debated his options. If he called the police, his family would die. He couldn't run; he didn't have a clue where he was. Again without choice, he returned to the safest location he could imagine, standing beside Mushey in the barn.

Clearly to the men in the barn, Kellestine was utterly devoid of both compassion and reason; Aravena was convinced now that he would meet the same end as Muscedere and Sinopoli. But he was not the only one terrified by the events unfolding: Aravena and MH both testified that Mushey had always had an air of confidence prior to this night, but even he wore his fear on his face.

All who were left inside the barn now of the Toronto Bandidos were the hangaround "Little Mikey" Trotta and the prospect Jamie Flanz, still endeavouring to clean up Raposo's blood on the barn floor, using brooms and blankets to steer the fluids into a crack in the cement.

Trotta was ordered to follow Kellestine. Aravena testified that Trotta enthusiastically jumped at the opportunity to finally go home and see his family and followed Kellestine out to the silver Infiniti. When he arrived there, one can only imagine what went through his head. Sinopoli's body weighed down the trunk and the hatch was open. Salerno sat lifeless in the rear. Trotta was ordered to climb into the passenger's side. This was not the home to which he wanted to return.

A gun had been pressed so hard against the side of Trotta's head that a mark was left. The bullet fired, travelling through his brain and out of the left cheek. He was also shot in the right chest; however, the bullet travelled no farther than muscle and soft tissue. He also suffered a bullet graze to his cheek just below his eye. No forensic experts could identify the type of ammunition used because it was so unusual. Perhaps it was one of the rusty bullets passed off in the toque the day before.

Throughout the insanity of the evening, Kellestine had indicated he was saving Flanz for last and the most vicious of attacks, alternately calling him a "fucking Jew" and a police informant. But who knew what would happen?

The last of the executed would not be led out to a vehicle by Kellestine as the previous six had. Instead, Sandham was to serve this order flanked by his Winnipeg brothers who had now all joined together outside to witness the evening's denouement.

According to evidence, Gardiner may have been outside as he had been ordered to remove items from the trunk of Salerno's Grand Prix and place them in the back seat of the car, some baby toys and an infant mobile. Must have been from Salerno's kid. Did Gardiner know yet why he was doing this?

More than likely, Gardiner would have been ordered back into the house after moving the toys.

Flanz was taken out to the rear seat of the Grand Prix. He would die alone in this vehicle without any of his brothers but surrounded by a child's toys as Sandham took his life with two rapid shots. Sandham eventually testified that Kellestine had ordered him to perform the execution and that when Sandham declined, Kellestine advised him that he didn't have much choice.

"If you don't do it, climb in the car, and I'll be right with you."

Again MH told the lie that Mushey had fired the second shot, something impossible from his position in the vehicle where he was merely trying to roll up windows. Forensic experts advised the direction of the bullets that killed Flanz had travelled from left to right, only possible from where

Sandham was standing, and fired by the gun on which all of his police training had been served.

MH said the gun that ended Flanz's life had jammed and that Sandham didn't know how to unjam it. But Sandham would never be caught in such a situation; his military and police training included unjamming this exact gun in the dark, blindfolded, in seconds flat. Moreover, Araveno's testimony, the most sincere of the lot, said the two shots were fired with rapid succession.

All of the Toronto vehicles now held at least one body, and, with the exception of the Volkswagen, had a driver's seat available.

The sun was rising on this Saturday, April 8, frost on the ground, mist in the air.

Kellestine ordered Mather to lead the convoy of vehicles out toward St. Catharines, a town southeast of London, which he presumably knew and might provide a dumping ground for the brothers.

MH indicated that he would drive the tow truck because he was the only one with the appropriate licence.

"I didn't want anyone risking a traffic ticket," he eventually told the courtroom.

The men in the vehicles could likely have just driven to a police station and reported the evening's events, but each of them could be certain that disobeying Kellestine's order would result in their deaths and the deaths of loved ones, if not by Kellestine, then by other 1%ers who could not let those live who had ratted on a brother.

Charged with the task of disposing of the bodies, all but Kellestine proceeded with the improvised interment along the 401, only turning off near Shedden when they realized one of the vehicles was running out of gas.

Another glitch in "the plan."

MH drove the tow truck. Aravena originally asked him if he could ride along with him, saying with a stutter that

MH not let them shoot his "pretty face" if he was going to be killed. MH merely laughed. Aravena was shaken and went to the silver Infiniti where Mushey had the driver's seat and he repeated the same sentiment.

Mushey didn't laugh. Instead he said that he would ensure they all made it out of there alive.

Mather drove and Gardiner took the passenger's seat in Flanz's rented Infiniti that now had the three bodies in it. MH followed with the tow truck and its cargo: one dead in the truck and three in the towed Volkswagen. Mushey and Aravena followed in Salerno's Grand Prix that had Flanz in the back seat; it was the car that didn't have any gas in the tank. Perhaps it was a good thing as the extra gas that sat in the can beside the car would be needed for the fire the next day to destroy the evidence.

Sandham drove his Jimmy behind them as he was their ride home.

When the cars were eventually ditched by the Steeles' home, with only Mushey bothering to actually park the car running on empty, Sandham sped off in the other direction, rather than waiting to drive them back.

He told the court that he considered going to the police. He told the court he considered going home. He told the court that if he did either, his family would be dead.

According to Sandham's testimony, he reconsidered and returned to pick up the men by the side of the road, who were clearly angered by his behaviour.

According to all other evidence, Sandham was a faker. He was a fake cop, a fake biker, and now a fake brother.

CHAPTER 12

Court, Crown, Chaos, and Celts

Talk of court news; and we'll talk with
    them too;
Who loses and who wins; who's in, who's
    out;
And take upon 's the mystery of things
As if we were God's spies.

              —*King Lear*, act 5, scene 3

The courthouse had designated a special elevator that only went to the floor of the Bandidos trial: the 14th. As per whatever superstitions preceded the creation of floors in a building, there was no 13th.

Triskaidekaphobia is the formal term for the fear of this number.

Thirteen has a special place in 1% motorcycle cultures, and a patch with the number 13 could adorn the front of a vest.

According to police specializing in motorcycle gangs, the 13 represents the 13th letter of the alphabet, *M*. To some it means "marijuana," to others it means "murder" and that only those who had committed a murder on behalf of the club could wear it. To still others who have been gang members it represents the number of steps to the gallows, where a brother would walk before he would talk.

Prosecuting attorneys are generally represented as polished executors of truth. Defence attorneys are the seedy folks who look for loopholes to get the guilty cleared of their accusations, and who feed off the misery caused by those who have committed crimes. The latter impression appeals to our sense of taxpayer money ill spent; the former appeals to a common sense that those who commit crimes must pay for their offences. It has always been easier to side with the Crown than the vagrants.

Did Wayne Kellestine deserve an attorney supplied by taxpayers? Most would say not. But he had his well-established team who had served him many times. Clay Powell was a man-about-town in London who had lived law all his life, even defending Rolling Stones member Keith Richards for a minor drug offence and serving on the prosecution team for the infamous Mount Cashel Orphanage physical and sexual abuse scandals in Newfoundland. That extensive investigation and trial sent him spinning into a deep depression that saw him hospitalized. When he returned to law, he refused to work in "the big league" and moved to London to have a quiet life. He now wrote a regular column for the local newspaper in which he mocked small-town philanderers and local politicians; he read extensively on the back deck of his Victorian home where he also tried to work through his personal relationships and philosophical quandaries, not easy on either front. He had defended Wayne on many occasions and even if there was no possible case for his client, he would stand by to watch his old biker friend go down.

Did Marcelo Aravena deserve a defence attorney who com-plained regularly in the elevator of the courthouse about "making only $100 per hour"? Most would balk at the complaint, but then expenses for a well-renowned downtown Toronto lawyer far exceed those experienced by some of the locals.

Michael Sandham was represented by a highly collegial team, but this was clearly a guy who needed more than a defence and midfield. By this point, the little man with more rationalizations than reconciliations needed a Hail Mary.

Dwight Mushey was served up by a superb defence team from Toronto. But Mushey was clearly the force with which the law would seek a reckoning. He demonstrated an ability to keep his cool and to keep his camaraderie. He would easily score in the top percentile of the population in terms of his intelligence with an athletic and spiritual force commanding respect from all, even if the journalists would peg him as a psychopath capable of killing anyone without batting an eye. Maybe he could be labelled a psychopath, but he had clearly been the one to understand caretaking of family and friends through the entire ordeal.

Frank Mather was represented by an interesting pair, his senior lawyer, Greg Leslie, stood about four foot eleven while the junior lawyer, Rob Lockhart, measured about six foot six. Despite his intelligence and research acumen, Lockhart did not have much experience in criminal law as his interests lay in environmental law; he would be happy to return to this when the trial was over.

Brett Gardiner was represented by Hicks, Block, Adams— a Toronto law firm built on the belief that any individual charged deserved the best defence possible, whether they be millionaires or homeless. Christopher Hicks had been a senior partner with the firm since its inception; a handsome, charismatic, silver-haired man who garnered respect from his Toronto colleagues and greetings from the crowd gathered to watch the trial. The local attorneys, however, regarded him less amicably with side comments about what they perceived as a self-aggrandizing deportment.

Indeed, he could easily be perceived an egotist, but he knew his law and worked tirelessly on Gardiner's behalf. Hicks had scores of murder trials under his belt as well as dozens of appeals going all the way to the Supreme Court, so even if he was periodically a bit condescending to the lawyers of London, he had earned the right.

The only female lawyers in the room stood out amid the grey hair and legal bravado. Kathryn Wells and Bella Petrouchinova each served as junior counsel respectively for Aravena and Gardiner. Serve they did, well beyond legal counsel as they stood in for the mothers and sisters who couldn't possibly excuse themselves from work for the many years these young men would serve before a verdict was rendered, a full three and a half years in detention.

Petrouchinova was in her late 20s, with a mere couple years out of law school but capable of following the preliminary inquiry with precision and dedication in the long hours of research that are required for such a complex case, sometimes incensing courtroom onlookers with her self-assured style. They couldn't know that over the three years she had bought Gardiner literally hundreds of books out of her own pocket and held a very special place in her heart for the young man.

The preliminary inquiry occurs before a jury is selected and it is here that case law is truly tested and ground rules for court are established. The prosecution has a chance to test its evidence and convince the preliminary judge that the case should go to trial. Similarly, the defence attorneys get to test their cases.

It commenced on January 9, 2007, in this special room on the "14th" floor, just a few weeks after the accused were able to read MH's submitted testimony. The preliminary inquiry was held under the highest security measures and a publication ban prevented journalists from writing about any evidence in the trial. They were merely able to report that Kellestine mouthed profanities at them and gave a courtroom artist the finger.

Though expected to last only three months, it did not end until June 21, 2007, two days after Gardiner's 23rd birthday, six months from its commencement. It was determined then that all six men would stand trial by jury.

Several months were now needed to prepare the legal cases and review the volumes of transcripts gathered during the preliminary inquiry.

Though Brett Gardiner was necessarily nervous, he placed full trust in his defence team. After nearly three years in detention in the Elgin-Middlesex Detention Centre in London, and after 12 jurors were selected from among 2,000 notices sent out and 125 people interviewed, Gardiner more than welcomed the beginning of his trial and hopefully the end of his ordeal. He had mellowed during his incarceration, shifting from being the "tough guy" he thought was expected, to being the guy who avoided trouble—not an easy position to assume in a highly volatile community of men.

Court commenced on Tuesday, March 31, 2009, with the opening remarks made by Mr. Justice Thomas Heeney, a middle-aged man with the thinning hair that one might expect of someone charged with such a challenging role at the head of the largest murder trial in Canada's history. His glasses perched easily on his nose, supported by the personality one would expect of a judge who had spent the necessary years perfecting his courtroom persona: superior, confident, intolerant of anything that might make the trial last longer than he thought it ought, but with an oddly feminine lilt in his voice.

With the opening of the case offered by Justice Heeney, the Crown began its arguments. The tension was palpable as the Crown Attorney for the County of Elgin, Kevin Gowdey, began; a man in his fifties with angular facial features, a receding hairline, intense eyes, and thin lips that in the medieval studies of physical features would have been associated with an articulate mastery of intricacies.

"Members of the jury, we finally begin. We'll be spending the next few months together with this case and out of those months I want to devote about the next two hours in making the Crown's opening comments to you today."

That opening address would span 55 pages of court transcripts, beginning by introducing the definitions of first-degree murder and moving fluidly through his opening address to the two key themes of the opening narrative.

"In the first part of our opening, I will tell you the story that brings us all here. In the second part, I'll be giving you a roadmap of sorts."

He began by introducing the eight men who died.

The slain men's wives, sisters, brothers, mothers, and fathers sat in the viewing area of the courtroom, their various emotions plainly set on their faces: sadness, anger, hope, fear. Some eyes were downcast, some glared at the men in the dock. Some hands fretted while others posed patiently. Some appeared to want retribution, others justice; some appeared to want hope, others closure and peace.

"At the end of this case, Justice Heeney will explain in detail that a single criminal offence can be committed by more than one person with each contributing in different ways." After proceeding through the evidence of what the police had witnessed at the Kellestine farm on the day of the arrests, he provided a caveat.

"I start with a word of caution. A trial with this number of people involved and the amount of evidence involved, does have some limitations. For all our strengths, our justice system has a shortcoming we need to acknowledge.

"One reality is that there's no opportunity for dialogue between you and counsel in the case. We may be leading evidence to prove something that you feel is perfectly obvious, but you must keep an open mind to the end, and you're not permitted to discuss the matter with us. You have been told and will be told again, that it's the Crown's obligation throughout the trial from beginning to end, to prove guilt beyond a reasonable doubt.

"What was motivating the people we are going to hear about? Who had what to gain and to lose?"

A very good question that applied to those prosecuting and defending the case, as well. The Crown prosecutors were surely elevating their careers by participating in the largest murder trial in Canada's history, and were likely aiming for loftier and more financially rewarding appointments to the bench. Some of the defence lawyers had virtually come out of retirement to represent the accused or decided to make the two-hour trek from Toronto, all on legal assistance that paid scanty sums. For various reasons, several judges declined to sit on this trial.

Gowdey continued with an overview of the evidence: guns, blood, phone calls, e-mail messages, and bonfire debris were placed as tantamount as well as a general indication of the number of expert witnesses who would eventually take the stand. Gowdey concluded by introducing the various members who would lead the Crown's evidence, a crescendo into his conclusion of the Crown's opening.

"Members of the jury, this is a big trial. Eight men were shot dead, one by one. Good or bad, nice guys or not, they never deserved that. Six men are charged with murdering them. When a crime is committed, whatever you may think of the victims or their lifestyle, the crime is committed against this community. You represent that community.

"After a very long process of jury selection, you have been chosen to be the judges of this case. These six men have placed their trust in the 12 of you. There's a lot to consider. It is serious work. We thank you in advance for your attention and the sacrifice that you will make for your community."

The 12 jurors, newly charged with their obligations, appeared collectively serious and sensitive, receptive, and perceptive.

The trial proceeded through the spring with forensics experts, motorcycle gang specialists, the Steeles and their discovery of the bodies, and numerous photos—in excess of 9,000 exhibits ranging from Bandidos vests, to the firearms located at the farm, through the many items found in the bonfire pit identifying keys and phones. There would be a total of 72 witnesses.

In mid-June, Mushey's lawyer had to forfeit his role as defence counsel due to a terminal illness in his family and the trial was put on hold. Though the Crown wanted to proceed as quickly as possible, Justice Heeney recognized that Mushey was one of the most seriously implicated and deserved to have time to find new representation. Moreover, the Crown's key witness, MH, was about to take the stand and Mushey's new legal counsel would need time to review the case and prepare. His new counsel, Michael Moon, would serve his client well as a potent, dynamic, and charismatic lawyer who would undermine MH's credibility in the months to come.

The wait for both MH and the men in the detention centre could not have been easy.

At least Kellestine was now joined by his old bank-robber buddy, Merv Breaton, who was now awaiting trial for trafficking. They could play cards and reminisce about the good old days.

• • •

The Elgin-Middlesex Detention Centre is poised unassum-
ingly in an industrial park located behind a large, brick government building where people get driver's licences and passports
renewed. A long stretch of paved road leads behind this to a
squat building that looks more like an elementary school built
in the 1960s than a penitentiary. Two rows of exceedingly
high fences, some 20 feet tall and topped with rolls of barbed
razor wire, surround the grounds, with video-security units
poised on posts, and sets of automatic gates, similarly high and
behind which sit an inmate transportation vehicle; of course,
the prisoner's compound would be housed somewhere in the
centre of the unit.

Several signs on the building reference appropriate clothing. No miniskirts, short-shorts, sheer tops, or T-shirts with
inappropriate language or symbols.

Visitors are greeted by a woman's voice via an intercom
by the door.

"Just a moment, please."

One must wait. One must give the name of the accused.
More waiting. And then, "Okay. Come in." The door immediately unlatches.

I try to enter, but the stern voice comes from within: "You
have to wait outside for Gardiner." The door again locks.

The voice eventually returns and the door is unlocked.
To the left a woman sits behind a glass veneer (presumably
bulletproof), much like the ticket booth at the movie theatre,
or an old bank where the teller sat behind a wicket. Here one
signs in with photo identification and must leave everything
in a locker before proceeding through the metal detector, and
the second latched door opens and closes with determination.

Once inside the facility the next door is heavy and painted
a bright orange. It's the entry to the visiting space.

Behind the orange door in a relatively nondescript room
with a central, glassed-in area, up to 26 visitors can sit on round

wooden bases, while within, men wearing orange shorts and T-shirts, white socks and black, slip-on shoes, which have the air of having been purchased in bulk from some Chinese manufacturer, perch on the same seats on their side of the glass. At each of the stations sits an aged black phone affixed to a metal box via a one-inch-thick metal cable and hardware that looks like it belongs on a washing machine instead of a phone. The phones have clearly been repaired on the cheap and duct-tape was not an option. Instead, there are retrofitted washers and screws. If one is lucky, the same phone is on the other side of the glass. With about 5 phones missing on the inside, only 21 visitors can speak to their friend or family member at any given time. In reality, probably only 15 of the phones actually work, and then only intermittently by banging them on their steel housing unit.

I had never been inside a jail and I wasn't even sure I would recognize Brett when he came to meet me. I waited uneasily.

When Brett finally arrived in the visiting area, he gently mocked me about my shaking hands. He was much calmer than I was and yet he had the most to lose talking to this "outsider."

Brett was anxious to share openly about his childhood and his interest in "the life," when and how it began; about finding his buddy Rich's dad in the Okotoks campground; about his drug use, his personal relationships, and some of his criminal activities. But never about the Bandidos or the murders.

For Mushey, he said, he would give his life and was certain that Mushey would reciprocate; this, despite experiencing a culture so volatile, and a brotherhood so tentative. That was all he revealed about his prime protector and would never speak of any of the others accused.

Despite the fact that he was never "in" the club, Brett could neither speak publicly nor testify as he would both be "out in bad" and have a lot of enemies if he did. He wanted "out in good."

He had received a letter from the mother of his girlfriend, someone who had now clearly wanted to support a transformation of the father of her grandson and who had been there for him from the time of his arrest. It was date-stamped April 9, 2009—three years after the day of his arrest—but he had only just received it on his 24th birthday on June 19th. The letter asked Brett to give up any pursuit of "the life."

Brett rhymed off the number of people he had trusted and followed as he considered whether he wanted to be a Bandido: the Preacher, a Bandido by the name of JB, and finally Dwight Mushey. His devotion to his girlfriends was equally unusual for a young man who had more than enough opportunities to be disloyal. He admitted to being possessive of his girlfriends, but he also became deeply and quickly attached to anyone he respected, even when they weren't necessarily deserving of his respect.

I didn't trust Brett after our first meeting. He seemed too quick to trust me. But I soon learned that Brett had no other motives in talking to me than sharing his story in the hopes that I might make a case why other young men should pursue a different life.

Brett was found to have many and diverse learning disabilities. He cannot listen to and retain information; he needs to read and reread it. His vocabulary is stilted, and he can't grasp basic mathematical concepts such as division and fractions.

When we met over the course of the coming months, Brett asked me about pronunciation and word usage. He wanted to improve his skills in reading and writing, having a new-found interest in poetry, journaling, and medieval runes. In turn I shared with him stories of King Arthur, the great Celtic leader, and King Lear, the tragic one.

Brett. Beau. Bull. In 24 years the young man with the doe-like eyes had experienced many transformations. From grade one failure, to grade seven bully, to big brother, to delinquent adolescent, to lanky Sea Cadet, to baptized, to Bandido hangaround, to inmate. Though he had a history of being lazy, he was growing more lethargic in the jail. He ate to provide himself some sort of comfort and wore his increasing weight around him as a shield. He learned to duck punches and insults hurled by fellow inmates. And, perhaps, less than being lazy, he had finally discovered that being a tough guy did not bring any rewards. Staying out of trouble was a necessity for survival.

During the last year of his detention, he ceased to want to be seen as the biker wannabe and he avoided any scenarios that might paint him as such. He wrote poetry for his girlfriend and son. He dedicated one of his poems to his sister, Sara.

A Brother's Tear

You my sister are a strong willed
Woman. I did not act like a big
Brother. More like your tormenter.

I should have been there when
You needed me the most, but instead
I took off to the coast.

It hurts me now when I sit
In my cell shedding a tear for
The way I treated you.

Now I live by the fear that I
Won't be seeing you for a while
Sitting in prison watching the
Charges pile up.

But now it's time to put that shit
Aside, because when you get married
I want to be by your side.
Remember, my baby sister, I love
You, and from now on I will be
There when you need me.

The book he treasured the most was a workbook that taught how to work with the spirituality of the runes in a Wiccan tradition. And he now defined himself with a new name, the ancient Celtic rune that eventually became the letter *B*. It was a rune representing rebirth, associated with the descent of an individual into some sort of a sanctuary where they would be reborn with a new sense of self. He was determined to turn his life around through this new-found spirituality.

He transcribed one of his Celtic prayers into the notebook he used to journal and write poetry.

> Oh ancient Gods of the Celts
> I call your presence here.
> For this is a time that is not a time,
> In a place that is not a place,
> On a day that is not a day.
> And we await you.

CHAPTER 13

A Brother by Any Other Name

Here I disclaim all my paternal care,
Propinquity and property of blood,
And as a stranger to my heart and me
Hold thee from this, for ever.

—*King Lear*, act 1, scene 1

Tensions mounted when the key Crown witness, MH, took the stand after months of forensic evidence. He was led through his "examination in chief" by the assistant Crown attorney, Tim Zuber. MH's answers were very short and his composure was intact throughout the entire examination. He provided details about the historic tensions between Winnipeg and Toronto, about Kellestine's and Sandham's travels to meet with American Bandidos. He provided names of other Bandidos who were not in attendance at the Kellestine farm that fateful April in 2006. And he provided a precise account of who shot whom and in what order. A remarkable feat of recall after more than three years, including details he was unable to provide in his initial evidence, as well as statements contradicting those made during the preliminary inquiry.

He began with Raposo, the adamant Torontonian with the cocaine addiction. Shot by accident by Sandham.

Muscedere, the most heroic of the group and the national president, was the first to be taken outside for execution. He had lived his life as a biker and was adamant that he would die a heroic death. After considerable defiance in the barn, he was walked out to the same waiting car in which Raposo's body had been loaded. Though in the preliminary inquiry, MH said he believed it was either Kellestine and Mushey, or Kellestine and Sandham, the story now changed in front of the jury. He was certain Kellestine led out Muscedere in the company of both Sandham and Mushey, with Mather picking up the rear. It was a whirlwind of accusations that the jury would not be able to comprehend. Mather sat, as always, stoic and somewhat dumbfounded in the prisoners' dock.

MH's confused testimony went unchallenged, and the reason he changed his story so many times was unexplored. After all, the Crown's mission was to have all of the men found guilty of first-degree murder.

After Muscedere left, MH testified that he heard the sounds of guns "popping" like popcorn. Perhaps because Kriarakis had been complaining about his abdominal wounds and was praying in Greek, he was the next to be led out.

MH said that Kellestine and Mushey accompanied Kriarakis out to the awaiting vehicle. This was unlikely given other testimony. By this point, Mushey seemed to have wanted nothing to do with the events of the evening. The only conclusion to be reached is that we do not know who witnessed his death, but it seems highly likely that Kellestine was again the one pulling the trigger.

The next to go out was Jessome. MH claimed to have gone out with Kellestine and Jessome, asserting that he did not know anyone was being executed. Once he told of witnessing the shooting, he said he realized what was happening that night and began to fear for his own life.

All testimonies indicated that Gardiner had never had a gun in his possession that night. He was the guy in the house monitoring the police scanner, but MH described him as far too lazy and unable to focus his attention to even contribute to this task.

Kellestine perched at the back of his box near the audience's entry and exit point, alternating between scribbling volumes of notes for his legal counsel. His hair had been shorn and he no longer stared down the media. He made no eye contact with MH though his strange coughing noises periodically resounded through the courtroom, sounding like a cross between a hyena and a horse.

The roll call continued.

According to MH, next out of the barn was Sinopoli, the 400-pound man with a wounded leg, forced to crawl into the trunk and shot there, allegedly by Kellestine and in the company of Mushey, but again MH's previous information put Sandham on the scene of this killing. And soon enough we would discover it was neither Sandham nor Mushey. Aravena would say he was the sole witness with Kellestine firing the gun.

According to MH, Salerno was next, followed by Trotta and Flanz.

As the last of the Toronto members exited the barn, everyone followed. Flanz had been the source of considerable abuse at the hands of Kellestine that night. All of the Winnipeg Bandidos were there to watch Sandham shoot him, and though MH would say that Sandham misfired and Mushey was the final shooter, the ballistics evidence would prove that the bullets entered from the side of the vehicle where Sandham stood. Apparently the first shot through the cheek was not successful in terminating the young man as Flanz, according to MH, "looked up and opened his eyes wide." The second shot through the forehead ended his life.

MH made a point of saying that Gardiner was still in the house when Flanz was shot.

With MH's roll call complete, it was now time for cross-examination by the defence team. Each senior counsel for each of the accused would come to the podium.

The first was Sandham's team of Crawford and Cudmore, who only managed to point out that MH had presented conflicting evidence about reaching Officer Tim Dyack.

Frank Mather's legal team focused heavily on the difference between a prospect and a probationary member. In the grand scheme of the charges, this seemed to be a point of little matter. It was important to raise, though, because only a patch member would be expected to kill. Their second line of argument focused on whether or not there were two additional Bandidos members at the farm that night since there had previously been reference to two Bandido Nomads coming up from the United States. It was clearly a point that deserved consideration since one of the farmers who had sighted the vehicles in the field on Saturday morning had also seen two men running away. All of the other men had been accounted for as they crammed into Sandham's SUV after ditching the cars that day. If there were Nomads there, one could be quite sure that anyone identifying them would be killed; Nomads were, after all, the elite, strategic "problem solvers." So it seemed best that the Crown forget about this potential evidence. It would just be too messy to try to get at the possible international connection. And this case was messy enough without it.

In a statement dated April 16, 2006, MH referred to the Nomads: "I didn't really get a good look at them." However, later in his original statement he clarified that they were not at the farm. That argument seemed to fall flat and if MH were lying, he was at least doing it consistently. Moreover, a private investigator hired by one of the defence lawyers indicated that Nomads were still south of the border, some five hours away, when the killings took place. Still, who were the guys running away in the field that morning? The farmers didn't have any reason to make that up.

Another theory was proposed: the two men running through the field were Hells Angels members. Again, MH wasn't going to give up anything to suggest this theory was correct.

Next came Tony Bryant, Marcelo Aravena's senior counsel. It was Thursday, July 24. The junior counsel for Aravena, Kathryn Wells, stepped up to one of the projectors and displayed an image on the screens throughout the courtroom of one of the murdered men as he was alive, a roguishly handsome Mediterranean fellow. Tony asked MH to identify him.

Q: Chopper?
A: Yes.
Q: Alive?
A: Yes.
Q: You didn't kill him, did ya?
A: No.
Q: Mr. Aravena didn't kill him, did he?
A: No.

Then Wells displayed a picture of Raposo as he was found in the vehicle.

Q: Dead?
A: Yes.

The line of questioning ambled on, but it would eventually have its desired effect. Wells put up the next photograph of a man smiling broadly, the one with a jester's face but a serious and respected reputation.

Q: Boxer?
A: Yes.
Q: Alive?
A: Yes.

The image of Muscedere came up on all of the screens with the once well-esteemed national president as he had been found on the morning of April 8, hours after he had smiled at Kellestine before the second bullet was fired into his head.

Q: It's a picture of Boxer, dead.
A: Yeah.

Exhibit 68C was next: a photograph of Kriarakis, the suave-looking, young Greek man.

Q: Crash, a picture of him alive, right?
A: Yes.
Q: Here's a picture of Crash, dead.
A: Yes.
Q: By gunshot. Did you kill him?

MH welled up with tears and shook his head.

Q: You didn't kill him, did you? That's a no, Sir.

Bryant paused as MH brought a tissue to his cheeks and composed himself.

Q: Not only did you not kill him, Mr. H——, you didn't plan on killing him either, did you?"

MH's teary response seemed to confirm that he had witnessed the execution. It was the reason his testimony was faulty in saying that Jessome died beside Muscedere, and it was the reason Jessome's blood was found by the DNA experts on the gun MH was holding at the time. If MH was crying so much now, might it be because he knew the next images to be presented would be of Jessome?

When the defence lawyers presented the theory that MH had witnessed Kriarakis's execution, MH denied that he had. Perhaps he had buried his offence so deeply in his subconscious that it was irretrievable, or perhaps he had been so well coached that he would never share his participation.

Regardless of what might have been coursing through MH's mind at the moment, he broke down and repeated his choked admission through tears.

"There was never a plan."

If this was the case, first-degree murder charges against the six men would rupture the Crown's case, since premeditation is the key element of first-degree murder under Canada's criminal code.

Bryant had exposed a slim but critical emotional fracture. It seems that for all their bravado, their donning of gloves, and their preparing of guns, none of them—not even Kellestine— had expected the evening to unfold as it had.

Eventually Bryant finished presenting the photographs of each of the slain. He counted each of them. Raposo, 1. Muscedere, 2. Kriarakis, 3. Jessome, 4. Sinopoli, 5. Salerno, 6. Trotta, 7. Flanz, 8. The graphic photos had caused some of the victims' family members to stumble out of the courtroom in tears.

The next photograph was of the stocky, dim-witted Chilean mixed-martial-arts fighter who was facing the charges of eight counts of first-degree murder while the man on the stand was walking free.

Bryant suggested that Aravena might have been number 9, and that MH might have been number 10. Though at first he appeared confused by the presentation of Aravena's image, MH came to understand.

"Nobody knew that night who was going to die, did they?"
MH wept in agreement.

Court was dismissed as MH was unable to continue. In fact, he was not capable of continuing the following day either.

Perhaps the Crown recognized that their story of Kellestine being in full control with a plan in place long before the murders was in jeopardy. Or perhaps MH really did need to go to the hospital the day after Bryant's cross-examination began given the considerable stress placed upon him. The unsavoury key Crown witness was falling apart.

When court resumed the following week, Bryant continued his previous line of questioning after he had referred to MH's emotional responses.

Q: You were afraid?
A: Yes.
Q: You were scared?
A: Yes.
Q: You were scared you were going to get done too?
A: At one point, yes.
Q: Yes? And, you were a person who was an officer of the Winnipeg Bandidos?
A: Yes.

Later in MH's cross-examination the jury would hear wiretaps with him on numerous occasions laughing because Aravena was scared that night also. As it turns out, he mocked fear in order to hide his own. As much as this 1%er culture tried to be countercultural, it continued to reveal itself as something tired and worn by intolerance. MH, Sandham, and Kellestine were not freedom fighters; they were anarchists devoid of ideology. More than anything, these were a bunch of boys who had not grown up to see the incongruities in their childhood games of cops and robbers. These men—these big, bad bikers—were ultimately terrified of each other.

Like the police, the public, and the media, everyone wanted to have a line drawn in the sand and a side to stand on. So fear could not be considered a factor.

Hicks was next to cross-examine. He had no need for anything aggressive since MH had clearly testified that Gardiner was not even aware of the killings. Hicks merely pointed out that Raposo was the secretary-treasurer who would have been receiving the Winnipeg dues and that since Raposo was an addict, it seemed likely that he was diverting funds for his own purposes. MH also affirmed that Kellestine had told him he used speed in the past.

It was the reason Kellestine had advised both his wife and one of the girlfriends on the phone after the killing: "I got fucked up and I fucked up."

The absence of a plan was further established by Hicks through a reference back to MH's initial interview with his handlers on April 16, 2006.

MH reported then, "I was under the assumption at one point that we're going to let them go. That's what I truly believed at one time. The next thing you know, he's [Kellestine] taking them out one at a time and they're not coming back. So 'cause he kept saying [that they were going to go home or to the hospital], I don't know how many times."

MH again confirmed that any one of the people at the Kellestine farm "could have been done that night." If Kellestine was not feeling the euphoric and superhuman effects of speed or coke or both, he was at least in some sort of a mindset that he was a god. After all, this was a man who would hold nothing back to have a chance to shock anyone who would pay attention to him, whether that meant picking up raccoon feces and eating it or suggesting that he would kill everyone and chop them up into little pieces for stew.

Despite providing damning testimony about the use of drugs by many of the men in attendance that night at

Kellestine's farm, the Crown's key witness also kept pointing evidence toward Mushey. But Hicks would let that go for now. His point was that Wayne Kellestine served divine providence that night while hopped up on speed.

Eventually, when the court witnessed Kellestine's arrest and his audio-video-recorded statement that night in the London jail, he spoke as an obsessive-compulsive, repeating himself frequently. He talked up a storm "more than [he] ever talked to a cop in his life," as he said over and over in the recording. He repeated that he had been partying all weekend, and admitted to doing drugs—referring to himself as a hypocrite for accusing the Toronto Bandidos members of doing the same. He phoned his wife, knowing full well that he was being recorded, and repeatedly claimed that the Hells Angels were responsible for the murders and that he was being framed; had he been "straight" that night, there is no way he would even suggest such a thing as he would surely be killed, either inside or outside of the jail for both betraying his own brothers and then accusing their greatest rivals. He told her he left his "script" for her, a reference likely to some drugs he had left at the house for her to pick up. Though the obsessive-compulsive banter was an indicator that he was likely still on speed, the arresting police officer commented that Kellestine "was completely sober." Clearly the Crown had a vested interest in such a position.

Perhaps the most telling point of Kellestine's frame of mind that night came after the police had asked for his shoes for forensic purposes. About five minutes after the police had taken his shoes, he looked down at his feet and stared for a solid 10 seconds.

"No shoes," he mumbled. He continued to stare down. "I gave them my fucking shoes." Again there was a rather comedic lapse and a shake of the head. "Why the fuck did I do that?"

The jury members laughed out loud.

After Kellestine had been charged and had some sleep, his appearance on audio-videotape the next day was far more exacting, though still repetitive. He now stated over and over that he would say nothing without his lawyer. Whatever drugs that had been in his system seemed to have left; however, he was clearly a demented man with many demons continuing to hover about him.

The suggestion that Kellestine was both in charge and stoned well beyond sensibility seemed a certainty, but nobody else tested the theory.

Hicks ended his cross-examination referring to the documents that MH had signed in order to be in witness protection and the Crown's obligation:

> To fairly assess [MH]'s sworn testimony obtained in the matter to referred to in paragraph 12, and his sworn testimony at trial or trials, of Messrs. Marcelo Aravena, Brett Gardiner, Wayne Kellestine, Frank Mather, Dwight Mushey and Michael Sandham, to decide whether the sworn testimony has been given in a substantially, complete and truthful manner.

Because MH said that Gardiner was only ever in the house monitoring the police scanner, his testimony was in effect Gardiner's potential salvation.

The most assertive of the cross-examiners was next. Michael Moon, Mushey's senior defence counsel, was a ruggedly attractive man in his 50s. Assuming the position of the previous lawyer called away by family illness, he had clearly done his homework and presented a force with which to be reckoned. He was going on full attack and bore his legal acumen and precision throughout the examination and began deliberately, aggressively, and precisely.

Q: I'm not interested in conversations. I'm going
to ask you a number of, I hope, fairly specific
questions that, for the most part, are going to
generate, ideally from you, a yes or no answer.
Do you understand that?"

A: Yeah.

Once Moon began, the Crown counsel interrupted a
number of times and the lawyer asserted his rights to have a
fluid interaction with the man on the stand.

> Your Honour, just before we start, I'm going to take
> some issue with any sort of speeches, objections by
> the Crown to which I believe is designed strictly
> to interfere with the flow of cross-examination. If
> they've got something merit-worthy to object about
> then they can stand up, but otherwise I think they
> should be quiet.

Justice Heeney agreed that those were the ground rules.

Moon moved gracefully through the construction of a
specific depiction of MH. First of all, he was a biker without
a bike. He had joined an elite, quasi-military club that was a
direct rival to the Hells Angels, even though he had previously
served the likes of the highest members of the Hells Angels.
He was a Bandido member who had sworn to the love, loyalty, and respect of his brothers even though he was a police
informant when he joined. He lied about income from drugs,
defrauding welfare, and even lying to his parole officer about
how much money he had made. As the sergeant-at-arms, he
was the one called to beat up anyone who was not following
club rules. The "loving smack," as it was called, would be done
at a church under orders of the president and he never had
shown reserve in hitting a man.

Moon then dwelled on the significance of brotherhood and camaraderie, the reason MH had joined the Bandidos organization. Because he had joined at the same time as Mushey, there should have been a special bond.

Q: Right. Yet, you were ratting them out from the very beginning?

A: Yes.

Q: You say that like it was nothing. Right?

A: It is what it is, it was, from the beginning.

Q: And you weren't ratting them out for money because you said you never got any?

A: Just at the end there.

Q: You weren't ratting them out to get a reduced sentence on anything because you didn't have any charges.

A: No.

Moon then proceeded to paint a less-than-appealing picture of MH as a husband and father. The jury learned that MH lied to his wife about the witness-protection program and how much money his family would make.

Q: So not only did you abandon your duty as a husband, you lied to your wife to bring her into the situation we're all in here today, right?

A: To get her to join the program?

Q: Yes.

A: Yes.

Q: You uprooted your kids, took them away from their lives, your wife away from her life, just so you could have them with you?

MH had an older child whom he had long ago abandoned, including any support or contact, and so Moon had successfully shown that MH was a liar and a fraudster with a long history of loathsomely selfish behaviour. Next he would prove that MH really didn't have any understanding of finances, deviating significantly in his statements that he made either $4,000 to $5,000 a month or $20,000 a day when he was a drug dealer. He further showed that MH never earned a living aside from his drug dealing, save collecting welfare and his disability income, even though he was going to the gym regularly with Mushey, lifting substantially heavy weights.

Then there was the presentation of some of the glaring differences between the first evidence provided, the preliminary-inquiry testimony, and the current trial testimony. MH reported that his memory had continued to improve since he had first sworn a statement, that he could recall much clearer three and a half years after the fact what had transpired that night. Wasn't it remarkable that he could remember better now than he could a week after the homicides?

Moon began to refer to him derogatorily as the "Rainman," an idiot savant. Despite all medical reports that MH was low functioning in terms of thinking and memory, he was adamant on the stand that everything he now said was truth. Nothing but the truth.

If that were indeed the case, why had his first statements not implicated Dwight Mushey? Why did Mushey become more and more culpable with each variation of testimony? Why did MH now weep when he spoke of his friendship such that court again needed to be recessed?

"Dwight," he sobbed uncontrollably through a tissue. "He was my friend." Another weekend off. Time to regroup.

In order to save his life he was committing a betrayal more bitter than any of the executions that had occurred that night at the Kellestine farm. Mushey was the most intelligent of the lot—capable of stealth, compassion, wisdom, insight, ambition—clearly a threat to the police force. Even if Mushey was never a ring leader, he was destined for such and had to be brought down before he could establish a presence. Why not use MH to cut the Bandidos off at the knees as well as the head? Take down Mushey so that he could never rise to the top.

Mushey remained stoic throughout MH's testimony, but he must have had feelings of anger and dismay regarding the disloyalty of one he had always protected. While many others in the organization had clearly ventured into a dangerous game of drug addiction, or played with other people's lives for their own selfish pursuits, Mushey never seemed to have had anything but the interests of his brothers at heart. Yes, he was criminally ambitious, but he was likeable.

For MH's negotiating immunity for involvement in the execution of eight men, Mushey's lawyer effectively pointed out that MH would have more than enough motivation to lie.

Q: You can lie through your teeth as long as you're not caught and you walk out of here, but if you're caught lying, then your agreement goes the way of the dodo, right?

A: Yes.

Moon then made the point that Sandham could never be trusted by MH and Mushey as his statements were often contradictory, self-aggrandizing, and put the members at risk. Sandham made up his own rules and changed them when it suited his needs.

Just as Hicks had established that Kellestine was a demented control freak strung out on speed, Moon demonstrated that the other leader on this night was similarly an egotist mad with power, even though perhaps fuelled by his own narcissism rather than precarious substances.

Kellestine was Hitler. Sandham was Napoleon. Anyone else charged was merely following the orders of their military leaders, lest they be killed themselves. But Mushey. He was a conundrum. He had potentially disobeyed orders yet had enough respect from others that he could get away with his defiance.

Mushey would not testify, Gardiner would not testify, Aravena definitely would, and Sandham would.

And Kellestine? Well, you just never knew what he would do.

CHAPTER 14

The wheel is come full circle.

—*King Lear*, act 5, scene 3

Criminal court is not nearly as engaging and condensed as popular culture presents. Most of the time spent is in tedious debate over the application of legal precedents.

The trial was winding up now on this special floor with a pre-charge hearing wherein the jury is excused and the judge offers up a draft "charge to the jury" that includes what evidence they should consider and what convictions are possible, and the lawyers debate the legal aspects of the final summary that the jury will hear and read. It is heavily influenced by the "factum," the submissions of each of the lawyers regarding precedents set by other legal decisions that should come to inform what the jury is charged with deliberating.

As the Bandidos murder trial was entering this final phase, numerous cases and questions arose specifically about what convictions were possible on each of the eight counts of first-degree murder. Each defendant would have to be separately considered for each count, but what might the convictions be?

The Crown had spelled out in its opening to the jury that there are two possible routes to consider whether or not a murder is "first degree": either it was pre-meditated or the murder happened while the person was confined.

Certainly first-degree murder for all eight of the slain was what the Crown desired for each of the accused, but the necessary balances of the judicial system must avail jurors to consider lesser charges. Second-degree murder, where pre-meditation has not occurred, was a possibility. A charge of manslaughter, which means that while a person has died the intent was not his death, only seemed plausible in the case of Raposo's death. But the Crown argued vehemently that in donning gloves and preparing guns, manslaughter was not an option because clearly the defendants knew there would be the potential killing of someone that night.

It came down to donning gloves? Why wouldn't the men put gloves on before touching any of Kellestine's weapons with their questionable histories?

The defence lawyers tried to argue that forcible confinement be one of the less serious charges considered; Hicks struggled to convince the judge that providing the range of forcible confinement scaling up to first-degree murder would provide the jurors with the greatest of options. He was not successful in having this potential conviction considered. It would need to be a point of appeal.

One of the other key legal issues raised regarded the two possible convictions of aiding or abetting or both. Such convictions were possible if an individual did not personally commit the act but was nevertheless involved in perpetrating the offence.

"Aiding" typically is affiliated in Canadian law with a direct action, while "abetting" is distinguished as the encouragement of the crime. Some debate ensued regarding whether the men walking behind the slain members were aiding and whether the donning of gloves and preparation of weapons could be considered abetting. Two appeal cases were called in to question this: one in which a man was found guilty for aiding when he held down the legs of a woman who was being killed, and another in which neither aiding nor abetting were suitable convictions for a man who stood by as a woman was raped by several men, his pants down around his ankles the whole time as he masturbated. He neither helped the perpetrators nor encouraged them, even though he found the sight erotic.

Finding an action morally offensive does not necessarily mean it is legally reprehensible. In the precedent case of the rape, the man was deemed to be neither aiding nor abetting. Aiding means an action is taken to support the crime. Abetting means verbal encouragement has been provided. Aiding and abetting have nothing to do with preventing a crime from being perpetrated.

Did aiding mean walking behind someone without the knowledge they would be killed?

It may seem legalese fodder, but it is significant in the heat of the moment whether knowledge of the crimes was held by those accused, remembering the limited chances for fight or flight and the greater likelihood of freeze that animals assume when the fear factor has struck.

The final major issue raised by defence attorney Michael Moon and supported by his co-counsel was whether the Crown attorneys were permitted to present a rather generic theory that *planning* had happened "at some point"—whether before leaving Winnipeg, during the weeks at the Kellestine farm, or throughout the evening of the slayings. Moon argued vehemently that the Crown must put forward a specific theory of what transpired to support a conviction of first-degree (premeditated) murder, including when the plans were set in place and who was knowledgeable about the plans.

If, for instance, the plan was formulated before the gloves were put on, then putting on gloves could be considered abetting. If, however, the plan only evolved after the shooting of Raposo, what happened before then could *not* be considered as part of a premeditated plan to murder. These nuances should have been spelled out in no uncertain terms to the jurors, according to Moon. But they were not.

The bottom line seemed to be that defence lawyers argued the object of the evening was a patch-pulling while the Crown argued that the object was murder, premeditated execution style of one chapter against another. The latter was all that the media would report.

After several trying days of legal argument, Justice Heeney had to retire to prepare his charge to the jury that would again be opened to the scrutiny of the now 18 lawyers before it was finally delivered to the jurors. The charge would necessarily be difficult and multi-faceted, and, as Moon pointed out, since jurors were not used to the work of lawyers "counting angels on the head of a pin," also had to be framed in a way that laypeople would understand. Justice Heeney had considerable work ahead of him.

At the beginning of the trial, defence attorney Clay Powell had suggested to the court that this case would not end until Halloween. The courtroom originally scoffed, but it seemed now, to the chagrin of everyone involved, that Powell's prediction some seven months ago was accurate.

As Justice Heeney prepared his charge, the attorneys prepared their closing arguments, and the accused grew anxious. It seems all but Kellestine still had some hope that "justice would be served," whatever that meant. Would the jurors understand the differences between first degree, second degree, and manslaughter? Would they be offered the chance to consider that some of the men were forced to contribute or be killed themselves—the legal argument of duress?

In a week, the jurors returned to their uncomfortable seats on the bench, one through twelve, six men and six women, ranging from young to middle-aged. The closing arguments came in.

Gord Cudmore, on behalf of Sandham, was particularly eloquent as he read his carefully crafted summation.

He painted a picture of Sandham as the boy who cried wolf, who because he had lied on so many occasions was not to be trusted in the end even if he was now telling the truth. And as he referenced the credibility of MH, he stated that "the truth did not set MH free; the telling of a credible story did." He also reaffirmed that "the smell of fear permeated the farm that night and the fear was not confined to the Toronto men."

Tony Bryant reminded the jurors that not only had Aravena provided the most sincere of the more than 70 testimonies during the trial, he had implicated himself in order to ensure that the facts be heard above the tales and webs of deceit that otherwise wove through the trial.

The other lawyers followed suit. Christopher Hicks, representing Gardiner, and Michael Moon, for Mushey, each referred to Kellestine and Sandham in fairly derogatory but certainly appropriate terms—as "monsters" and "psychopaths."

Powell, representing Kellestine, derided the apt representations of the Toronto-based lawyers for Aravena, Mushey, and Gardiner as the mere haberdashery of "Bay Street Thumpers." Some derogatory term that perhaps would resonate with the much smaller town of London.

The onlookers in the court gallery chatted among themselves: Why hadn't Kellestine taken the stand? As a biker in his mid-60s and with the certainty of death in the penitentiary either by the hands of time or other inmates, he could have admitted his culpability and saved a few brothers.

But then, they conjectured, he never really cared about brothers, did he? And it seems his defence counsel was equally dismissive of the men in the dock. Moreover, there remained the suspicion that he had been protected by the Hells Angels and would continue to be when he entered the penitentiary.

Without Kellestine's admission of guilt, Mushey and Gardiner needed to fire their senior defence lawyers. It was difficult for most to fathom, but if they faced time in a penitentiary, they could not afford to be affiliated with lawyers who had mounted an attack on another biker, no matter how deserved the criticism was.

It's tough to root for guys who won't speak up for themselves in the courtroom and then have the audacity to fire the very lawyers who have fought for years for them. But you have to understand the inside of the system. Had Gardiner and Mushey permitted their lawyers to slander Kellestine, they would be deemed "rats" for permitting their defence to speak ill of another brother. If they didn't fire Moon and Hicks, they would be facing very hard times when they went to jail: protective custody, solitary confinement, 23 hours per day locked in a cell.

Mushey, Gardiner, and Mather remained chummy throughout. The accused knew all too well what life was like on the inside and that they needed to protect themselves and each other. They knew well enough that Sandham and Aravena couldn't be counted in their circle since they had taken the stand. Kellestine had long ago deserted them.

The judge's charge to the jury following the closing statements seemed to suggest that Gardiner might have a chance at freedom.

The charge included the following statements:

> If you find that Gardiner's state of mind changed when he heard the shots that killed Muscedere, the

Crown will have to prove that Gardiner did some further act of aiding or abetting after that point in time, knowing that someone was going to get killed and intending to help or encourage that killing. The only evidence of words or actions on the part of Gardiner after Muscedere was killed was moving articles from the trunk of Flanz's car to the back seat. Given that Flanz was, on the evidence, shot in the back seat, not the trunk, it is for you to say whether that act, if you accept that it was done, actually helped to facilitate the killing or encourage it, and that it was done with the intent required for murder as I have described it above.

On the concept of duress, Heeney ruled as follows:

You have heard evidence from Aravena that Kellestine threatened to kill Aravena and his family if he told anyone what he had seen. You heard evidence that Aravena was afraid he might be the next to be killed. Sandham also testified that he thought he was going to be killed if he did not do what he was told by Kellestine, and was explicitly threatened that if he did not shoot Flanz, he could get in one of the cars himself and Kellestine would be "right with" him. If, after the analysis I have just instructed you to go through, you find that either one of them committed, aided or abetted in any murders, you might wonder whether it matters that he may only have participated in those murders because he thought he might be killed himself if he did not. The short answer is that it does *not* [author's emphasis] matter. A threat or an implied threat engages the concept of duress where, under certain strict conditions, a person is excused from having committed a crime if he only did so under a threat of death or serious bodily harm. Duress is not available as a matter of law to a charge of murder, and for other legal reasons which I need not get into, it is entirely irrelevant to this case. In a nutshell, it is not open to anyone to say to an innocent victim "you will die so that I can live."

This point was drawn out in paragraph 74 of the charge:

So a person who aids or abets in a murder, while operating under a threat, may well not desire the outcome, and may not want anybody to die. But as I have just instructed you, "intent" is not equated with "desire." So long as he knew a murder was about to be committed, and chose to do acts that he knew would help or encourage the perpetrator to commit that murder, that is sufficient to make him guilty of murder as an aider or abettor. Whether or not he did those acts under threat, and whether or not he wanted anybody to die, is irrelevant to your task.

Such an interpretation of the law would have to be a major contention for appeal.

The jury had 139 pages of judge's charge to consider in their deliberations, highly nuanced in terms of the kinds of evidence they might consider and the special applications of law, especially as concerned the concepts of aiding and abetting.

As the jurors exited the courtroom for deliberations, with a charge that clearly supported Gardiner's potential innocence and a series of closing arguments by the defence team that supported such a position, it seemed possible that they would return after several days of deliberation with a decision that would help him turn his life around. They had nodded to the many suggestions that Gardiner was the least culpable of the lot, a young man who had been duped into believing that he was going to receive the respect he felt he had missed throughout his life.

The judge's charge had, in effect, specified that an individual must knowingly be participating in the offence of murder in order to be convicted and had explicitly provided Gardiner as an example where such might be questioned.

The jurors elected their lead and were provided a decision tree to help them reach their conclusions. It's a simple chart for the jurors to record their decisions for each of the accused on each of the counts that could now range from first-degree murder to second-degree murder to manslaughter. Forcible confinement was not an option on the tree.

Whatever happened in that juror's room we can never know because of the laws protecting the secrecy of a jury's deliberations. There were many forces with which the jurors had to reckon.

They faced a high-profile case in which most of the public would assume guilt from the onset. All jurors are free to walk about the streets until the final charge is delivered and they are sequestered. So, this was the first time in those many months that the jurors would not be exposed to the dominant opinions of the public and the press.

Bikers killing bikers. Who cares? Well, likely other bikers would, both inside and outside the jails.

The trial took seven months, the charge itself had taken two days in court, yet the verdict was reached within a mere 14 hours of deliberation for 48 counts against six men resulting in a series of condemnations that would cost six men their lives.

Michael "Taz" Sandham: *eight counts of first-degree murder.*

Marcelo "Fat Ass" Aravena: *one count of manslaughter and seven counts of first-degree murder.*

Frank Mather, who never even had a Bandido name: *one count of manslaughter and seven counts of first-degree murder.*

Dwight "D" Mushey, the one who was not even in the barn when the first shots were fired: *eight counts of first-degree murder.*

Wayne Kellestine: *eight counts of first-degree murder.*

Brett "Bull" "Beau" Gardiner: *two counts of manslaughter and six counts of first-degree murder.*

MH: *free, a new identity for himself and his family, and money for life.*

As the jury lead read out the convictions, Aravena lost his temper, yelling at the jurors and threatening his senior defence counsel. One of the jurors wept and trembled. Aravena had, after all, provided them the most sincere account of what had transpired over three years ago and had, as a result, signed his own death sentence if not a minimum of 25 years in protective custody that translated to 23 hours a day locked in a cell. For stepping forward and telling the truth, he was now a "rat" according to prison culture and certainly would not have the luxuries that were afforded to MH.

Perhaps the crying juror knew that she was ending a man's life. Seven months of testimony with gruesome details. It's a wonder more of the jurors weren't crying.

"I want everyone to understand that biker gangs are inherently violent and I think that this trial has given us a glimpse into that lifestyle of the motorcycle gangs," reported OPP Detective Inspector Paul Beesley as he contextualized Aravena's violent outburst to the media.

But Aravena was just expressing the fear that bikers aren't allowed to express. He was naive in thinking that his testimony would be understood as his grade-five mind worked.

You could see a frustrated boy. "I'm telling the truth."

"I had to help clean up or I would be dead."

As his temper flared, most would only see a dangerous man rather than a confused boy in a man's body.

The jurors were excused following their verdict and did not get to see Aravena's tearful lament the following day in which he extended a heartfelt apology to the families of the slain following the readings of their victim-impact statements. Gardiner similarly bowed his head and apologized. None of the others who had been convicted spoke.

Jurors are excused from the theatre before the final act, the one in which the true tragedy is exposed.

The reports that rang out throughout the globe claimed that justice had been served as the parents reading the papers and watching the news prepared their children for a night of trick-or-treating.

It was, after all, just one more headline about a bunch of bikers killing bikers.

Each of the convicted faced an absolute minimum of 21 years in prison before they could even request a parole hearing, and Gardiner was a mere 25 years old when the sentence was pronounced.

•   •   •

On the Stafford Line, as the trial came to a close, one simple white cross remained with a Greek orthodox design and a crown of plastic greenery. Above the crown, in black marker were the words, "RIP ALL." Another rough-hewn and aged plank of broken barn board is still nailed to a fence post with another message in black marker, practically carved into the wood: "Depart. Missed" The rest of the barn board monument had been wrenched away.

The slight blue spruce tree and mums planted some three and a half years ago to mark the loss are also gone, as is the Maple Leafs hockey jersey.

An unwitting monument to a story that has proven insignificant to most, curious to some, and tragic to few, any onlookers can now only speculate about the rest of the barn-board plank's message.

At one time, perhaps it said "Brother."

Epilogue

I am a man
More sinn'd against than sinning.

—*King Lear*, act 3, scene 2

In the days following the trial, an air of resolution and peace seemed to settle around Brett.

"I'm glad it's over with," Brett said solemnly when I met with him one last time at the detention centre following the conviction.

He was also relieved that the new Canadian legislation that prevented those convicted from serving time concurrently had not been passed before he was brought to trial. Had that law been in place, Brett would be facing his entire life in prison, instead of most of it.

I saved my tears and anger for the car ride away from London. Brett didn't need to see any of that.

At least two of the convicted (Aravena and Sandham) would now be labelled rats and need to go into protective custody for the duration of their sentences. All of the convicted prepared themselves for what they were told would be a long haul through months of assessment at the high-security Millhaven Penitentiary in Ontario, and the following months or years before they might actually arrive at locations where family could access them.

Hard to say whether Wayne Kellestine would be embraced, feared, protected, or murdered. But then, he was always a survivor. Chances are that if he really wanted to stay alive, he wouldn't be able to stay in the general population. Especially in Millhaven's J-Range, one of the toughest ranges in the whole Canadian system and heavily populated with 1%ers of various affinities.

Frank Mather longed for the Atlantic shores of his New Brunswick home while Dwight Mushey and Brett Gardiner hoped they might continue their camaraderie in a penitentiary out West, hopefully in Alberta. There were a few benefits awaiting them as they prepared to leave the London detention centre that had been their home for well over three years. They would be permitted their own clothing and shoes, their own televisions and Sony Playstations with a maximum of 20 games, and a CD player with the same maximum number of CDs. They would be able to further their educations finally, have access to fitness facilities and a library, and eat better food. But all this was paid at the price of spending the next several years in virtual confinement and only escaping that significant constraint if their security assessments eventually permitted them.

Mather's girlfriend, Kelly, was preparing to marry him now. Eventually he would be entitled to conjugal visits and to be able to hold his child.

Before they left London, Aravena moved into protective custody in the same cell as Sandham.

Not surprisingly, the blogs on the various news sites reported celebration over the outcome while wishing that the taxpayers should be saved a few dollars with the reinstatement of capital punishment. Special security, a judge, six Crown attorneys, 12 defence attorneys, court staff, a minimum of 15 police officers in the courtroom through the entire preliminary inquiry and trial by jury. Taxpayers had literally spent millions of dollars on their convictions.

The Gardiners went about making the plans necessary for purchasing and transporting the allowable possessions Brett would need to see him through the next few years in Ontario, doing so with the same detached sense of reality one experiences when making funeral arrangements for a loved one. He was supposed to go to Millhaven, but a sudden change resulted in him being transferred to the Edmonton Institute. Solo.

Dwight Mushey was taken away from him and sent to Prince Albert.

Sandham and Aravena wound up in Winnipeg and Mather in New Brunswick.

Though their legal rights should have ensured them an assessment prior to placement, apparently none of them warranted that, a mirror of their lives.

In Canada, anyone who is found guilty has a right to have the case reviewed at a higher level court. Since there is an automatic sentence for first-degree murder, the sentence could not be appealed. The legal teams would instead appeal the actual conviction.

Appeals were filed by each of the convicted shortly after the trial had ended. First came the notice of appeals, two-page summaries of the rationale for a higher court to review rulings.

Only the application of law is reviewed, which means that lawyers contend precedents and the interpretation of the law.

Following the submission of a notice of appeal, lawyers must file further documents that designate the specific cases before the appeal process can begin. The appeal book submitted by both the appellant (in this case, defence counsel) and the respondent (the Crown counsel) would also require all transcripts and evidence.

In the case of those who have undergone a trial together, all appeals are reviewed at the same time.

Gardiner's lawyers filed all of the necessary documents on time. Such was not the case for the others convicted. Close to a full year passed before all notices of appeal were submitted.

Brett's sudden arrival at Edmonton had his parents scurrying to secure his television, clothes, movies, and CD and DVD player since a convicted person can only have one delivery of his property within a few months of his arrival in the penitentiary.

They filed their papers to visit. Brett's mom was denied visiting rights for three months. None of his family members would be able to see him at Christmas.

Because of his affiliations with the Bandidos, Brett was assaulted shortly after his arrival. As a result of the attack he had a broken jaw that needed to be wired back together with a steel plate installed; he had also been stabbed several times by a pen that punctured his lung. It seems some folks didn't like the fact that he had associated with the Bandidos, albeit peripherally. And since he was never even a member, he had no one inside to watch his back.

As Brett settled into his new home, he restored his relationships with Regan and their son. They could finally touch each other after four years.

He entered into a part of the penitentiary in which only those recovering from gangs could be located. To get in, he had to prove that he was serious about getting his life back. The first tattoo to go was the Bandidos logo.

He had no contact anymore with any of those convicted, save to hear that Mather did get married.

The appeal requests for all of the convicted were eventually filed.

Canadian law previously granted automatic appeals to anyone who was convicted of first-degree murder. But times have changed and budgets are tighter. In the fall of 2010, a committee was struck by Legal Aid, the public body that provides defence counsel to those who cannot afford it. They are to decide whether or not public funds should be spent on the appeal. After all, millions of dollars were already spent on the preliminary trial and the trial itself. Did we want to be spending more of the taxpayers' money?

Over a year after the appeals were filed, in February 2011, Legal Aid determined that appeals would be permitted for only three of the convicted: Gardiner, Aravena, and Mather. But the court reported that transcripts for the appeals would not be available until December 2013.

After Brett spent a couple of years in the penitentiary under conviction, his girlfriend went her own way. She needed to work at restoring life for her and her son without the glare of the attention necessarily associated with such a tragedy. Because of good conduct, Brett would soon be moving to a medium-security penitentiary closer to his family in Calgary. Mushey was also slated to move to a medium-security facility, potentially the same one.

Kellestine is still alive as I write these final notes. Word on the street is that he was never and would never be safe. But word on the inside is that he will die of cancer, alone and in segregation, likely before this book is published.

As I sit writing this epilogue so long after the murders and trials, I revisit my own challenges in writing this book. Many friends have asked if I fear for my life at the hands of bikers. I do not. I have instead feared a system wherein those who come before it are assumed guilty and need to be proven innocent.

But fear isn't the dominant emotion as I scribble these last few lines. Instead, I have hope. Hope that those who met me and wondered why on earth I would ever undertake this project can now say:

"I get it."

INDEX

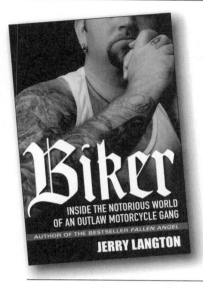

Biker
by Jerry Langton

The first book in the Ned Aiken series, featuring his life in the criminal biker brotherhood.

You'll never meet the bikers in this book or visit the mythical rust-belt city of Springfield. But through the eyes of Ned "Crash" Aiken, you will experience the real world of the outlaw biker gang—a world shaped by desperation, casual brutality and fascinating rites of passage. *Biker* follows the career trajectory of "Crash" from his days as a small-time high school drug dealer to his rapid rise through the ranks of a biker gang that is rapidly and brutally expanding its territory and criminal connections.

Aiken's story relates how an outlaw biker sees his gang from the inside. It is an experience shaped by seamy and ruthless characters waging a never-ending battle to establish their supremacy. From drug running and gun sales, to prostitution and allegiances forged by violence, this is a struggle played out within biker gangs the world over. And as the reader discovers in this intense docudrama, this is not the romantic freewheeling beer-fest version of the Hells Angels, but a sleazy existence that draws social outcasts like moths to a flame.

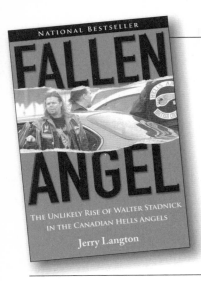

Fallen Angel
by Jerry Langton

The unlikely rise of
Walter Stadnick in the
Canadian Hells Angels

Walter Stadnick is not an imposing man. At five-foot-four, his face and arms scarred by fire in a motorcycle accident, he would not spring to mind as a leader of Canada's most notorious biker gang, the Hells Angels. Yet through sheer guts and determination, intelligence and luck, this Hamilton-born youth rose in the Hells Angels ranks to become national president. Not only did he lead the Angels through the violent war with their rivals, the Rock Machine, in Montreal in the Nineties, Stadnick saw opportunity to grow the Hells Angels into a national criminal gang. He was a visionary—and a highly successful one.

As Stadnick's influence spread, law enforcement took notice of the Angel's growing presence in Ontario, Manitoba and British Columbia. However, Stadnick's success did not come without a price. Arrested and charged with 13 counts of first-degree murder, Stadnick beat the murder charges but was convicted of gangsterism and is currently serving time.

Fallen Angel details one man's improbable rise to power in one of the world's most violent organizations, while shedding light on how this enigmatic and dangerous biker gang operated and why it remains so powerful.

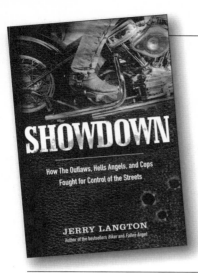

Showdown
by Jerry Langton

Control of Ontario's underworld wasn't decided in a day, a year, or any single event. It was a series of skirmishes, bloodbaths and blunders.

When the old-school Mafia in Hamilton fell apart following the death of Johnny "Pops" Papalia, a frenzy ensued for who would control Ontario's drug and vice traffic. The leader of the Hells Angels, Walter Stadnick, had had his eye on Canada's most lucrative drug market for years but had been kept out largely due to the mafia syndicate that only reluctantly employed bikers of any stripe for their dirty work, and Papalia's refusal to use any Hells Angels.

The war to fill the power vacuum in Ontario would hinge on the broadly supported Stadnick's Hells Angels, a handful of smaller clubs too proud or too useless to join them, and Mario "The Wop" Parente's Outlaws, the top motorcycle club in Ontario since the 70s. Other challengers would emerge from the ever-shifting allegiances of the biker world, including the Bandidos from south of the border, whose presence in the province would end in a bloodbath now known as the Shedden Massacre. Against all of these competing interests stood the various law enforcement agencies responsible for keeping the general peace and shutting down as many operations as they could.

Rage
by Jerry Langton

Sibling violence may be as old as time, but this case is particularly disturbing and unsettling.

In a quiet working-class neighborhood in east-end Toronto, on an early winter day in November 2003, Johnathon Madden returned home from school only to be bullied and threatened by his older brother, Kevin; Kevin's friend Tim Ferriman; and another teenager. The confrontation turned violent and fatal. Johnathon didn't have the strength or size to protect himself against the frenzied attack of his powerful 250-pound brother.

Kevin Madden had problems. This was not news to his family, teachers, principal, social workers, and psychiatrists. But what drove him to commit murder—and why Johnathon? Why were his friends compelled to take part in the bloodletting? What events were going on behind the scenes that played a part in the tragedy?

Jerry Langton sets out to answer these questions and look for the clues that drove Kevin Madden over the edge. His investigation takes him onto the streets of Toronto, where he unearths a disturbing teen subculture, into cyberspace, and into the confidence of neighbors and students who knew the Madden family. Langton reveals shocking testimony from the trials—one of which was declared a mistrial due to the perjury of a witness—and exposes the twisted lives of youth living in a parallel universe where death is met with complacency.

Gangland
by Jerry Langton

A startling look at Mexico's new power elite—the Mexican drug cartels.

Gangland is a first-hand examination of the rise of the Mexican drug cartels, and traces their origins, evolution, and how they've grown in lock-step with the failed narcotics policies of North America. Warring amongst themselves as much as with the authorities, the cartels have earned their reputation for violence and intimidation with daylight gun battles, corpses hung from overpasses and coolers full of severed heads. Their power has escalated thanks to a police force that's often seen to be corrupt or incompetent, a government barely in control of itself, and military personnel serving within their own borders who must cover their faces to keep their families safe from the long, ultraviolent arm of the cartels. Stuck in the center of this maelstrom are the vast majority of Mexican citizens seeking only peace, prosperity and security, and finding little to none in their homeland.

Two questions dominate Mexico's drug war: Who's in charge, the government or the cartels? And how deeply have the cartels infiltrated the United States and Canada? One thing is clear: the War on Drugs has failed, and soon, so may Mexico.

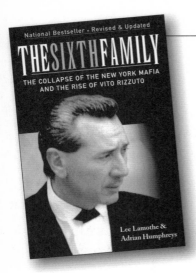

National Bestseller · Revised & Updated

THE SIXTH FAMILY
THE COLLAPSE OF THE NEW YORK MAFIA
AND THE RISE OF VITO RIZZUTO

Lee Lamothe &
Adrian Humphreys

The Sixth Family
by Lee Lamothe &
Adrian Humphreys

"A briskly written and timely story of the rise and apparent fall of the Rizzuto crime family in Montreal, with enough blam-blam to keep true crime buffs turning the pages."

—*The National Post*

"[*The Sixth Family*] is essential reading, not only in the context of the looming Rizzuto murder trial, but for anyone concerned about the intrusion of traditional organized crime into every facet of our society."

—*The Globe and Mail*

"With a reporter's eye for detail and a novelist's gift for storytelling, the two authors lay bare the Rizzuto family's inner workings and international connections."

—*The Record* (Kitchener)

The Weasel
by Adrian Humphreys

"I started small in the mob and stayed small."

— *Marvin Elkind, a man known as The Weasel*

In the world of organized crime the bosses grab the headlines, as the names Capone, Gotti, Bonnano, Cotroni and Rizzuto attest. But a crime family has many working parts and the young mobster known as The Weasel was the epitome of a crucial, invisible cog—the soldier, the muscle, the driver, the gopher.

By a quirk of fate, Marvin Elkind—later The Weasel—was placed in the foster home of a tough gangster family, immersing him from the age of nine in a daring world of con men, cheats, bootleggers, loan sharks, bank robbers, leg breakers and Mafia bosses. During a Golden Age of underworld life in New York, Detroit and across Canada, The Weasel found himself working with a surprising cast of colourful characters. But his disenchantment with the broken promises of mob life brought him into another fraternity, one offering the same adrenaline rush, danger and dark comedy he craved. After a startling confrontation, he was embraced by law enforcement, and a cop with a reputation for results. Now a career informant, The Weasel learned he was a far better fink than he ever was a crook.

With his impeccable gangland pedigree, enormous girth, cold stare and sausage-like fingers adorned with chunky rings, no one questioned The Weasel's loyalty. The backroom doors were flung open and The Weasel slipped in, bringing undercover cops with him. For case after case over two decades, he worked for the FBI, U.S. Customs, Scotland Yard, RCMP, Ontario Provincial Police and other law enforcement agencies on three continents, trapping and betraying mobsters, mercenaries, spies, drug traffickers, pornographers, union fat cats and corrupt politicians.

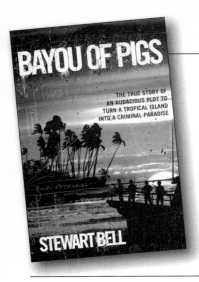

Bayou of Pigs
by Stewart Bell

The true story about an
idyllic tropical island and the
mercenaries who set out to
steal if for profit and adventure.

In 1981, a small but heavily armed force of misfits from the United
States and Canada set off on a preposterous mission to invade an
impoverished Caribbean country, overthrow its government in a
coup d'état, install a puppet prime minister, and transform it into
a crooks' paradise.

Their leader was a Texas soldier-of-fortune type named Mike
Perdue. His lieutenant was a Canadian Nazi named Wolfgang
Droege. Their destination: Dominica.

For two years they recruited fighting men, wooed investors,
stockpiled weapons, and forged links with the mob, leftist revo-
lutionaries, and militant Rastafarians. They called their invasion
Operation Red Dog. They were going to make millions. People were
going to die. An entire nation was going to suffer. All that stood in
their way were two federal agents from New Orleans on the biggest
case of their lives.

Set in the Caribbean, Canada, and the American South at the
beginning of the end of the Cold War, and based on hundreds of
pages of declassified US government documents as well as exclu-
sive interviews with those involved, *Bayou of Pigs* tells a remarkable
tale of foreign military intervention, revolutionary politics, greed,
treachery, stupidity, deceit, and one of the most outlandish criminal stunts ever conceived: the theft of a nation.

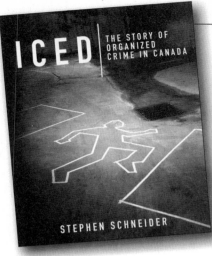

Iced
by Stephen Schneider

"You're lucky he didn't have an ice pick in his hands. I know how this guy performs."

— *Mobster Paul Volpe speaking about a Buffalo-mafia enforcer named "Cicci"*

Iced: The Story of Organized Crime in Canada is a remarkable parallel history to the one generally accepted and taught in our schools. Organized crime has had a significant impact on the shaping of this country and the lives of its people. The most violent and thuggish—outlaw motorcycle gangs like the Hells Angels—have been exalted to mythic proportions. The families who owned distilleries during Prohibition, such as the Bronfmans, built vast fortunes that today are vested in corporate holdings. The mafia in Montreal created and controlled the largest heroin and cocaine smuggling empire in the world, feeding the insatiable appetite of our American neighbors. Today, gangs are laying waste the streets of Vancouver, and "BC bud" flows into the U.S. as the marijuana of choice.

Comprehensive, informative and entertaining, *Iced* is a romp across the nation and across the centuries. In these pages you will meet crime groups that are at once sordid and inept, yet resourceful entrepreneurs and self-proclaimed champions of the underdog, who operate in full sight of their communities and the law. This is the definitive book on organized crime in Canada, and a unique contribution to our understanding of Canadian history.